THE GOLDEN CORRAL

THE
GOLDEN CORRAL

*A Roundup of Magnificent
Western Films*

by
ED ANDREYCHUK

McFarland & Company, Inc., Publishers
Jefferson, North Carolina, and London

Front cover: Ben Johnson, Warren Oates, William Holden, and Ernest Borgnine are ready to face the Mexican general Mapache in *The Wild Bunch* (1969)

British Library Cataloguing-in-Publication data are available

Library of Congress Cataloguing-in-Publication Data

Andreychuk, Ed.
    The golden corral : a roundup of magnificent Western films / by Ed Andreychuk.
        p.   cm.
    Includes bibliographical references and index.
    ISBN 0-7864-0393-4 (sewn softcover : 50# alkaline paper)
    1. Western films — History and criticism. I. Title.
PN1995.9.W4A63   1997
791.43'6278 — dc21   97-21512
                                                                      CIP

Manufactured in the United States of America

McFarland & Company, Inc., Publishers
  Box 611, Jefferson, North Carolina 28640

*Dedicated to my wife, Marcia,
and our daughter, Kristin*

CONTENTS

ACKNOWLEDGMENTS

Many thanks...

To the Anne Arundel, Baltimore, Harford and Howard County (Maryland) library systems, and to the Enoch Pratt Library System in Baltimore City (particularly their central branch), for the books, magazines and newspapers they provided for research.

To Eddie Brandt's Saturday Matinee, Cinema Collectors, and Larry Edmunds Bookshop (all in California), and to Jerry Ohlinger's Movie Material Store (in New York), for the wonderful stills.

To all the studios originally releasing the 14 Western films featured, as well as all those responsible for the later home video versions.

Most of all, to every filmmaker who was involved in bringing these Westerns to the screen.

INTRODUCTION

My love for Western films began in my boyhood, thanks to my father, who took me to see them because he loved them, too. I was nine years old when he took me to see *The Alamo*. This film, more than any other, opened my heart to the Western genre just as it opened my eyes to those enormous vistas on the screen. I was drawn to Westerns, not only by the entertainment they provided, but by the allure of the spirit they portrayed — a spirit of great courage and perseverance in a land both beautiful and brutal.

The Golden Corral is a work of reflection, an examination of fourteen exceptionally fine Western films in terms of their entertainment and historical value. This includes their value not only as part of the motion picture industry, but as part of the American cultural landscape, offering a perspective on the nation's ideals as they were expressed in the legends of the Old West.

Coverage of each film begins with credit and cast lists and a synopsis of the storyline. A full discussion of the film follows the synopsis, offering background information, production details, and an analysis of plot and thematic elements.

Each of these films features some plot elements based on historical fact. For this reason, each film is examined, to some degree, in light of actual history and the real lives of men and women of the Old West. But it isn't really important that filmmakers sometimes took liberties with historical fact. Purists may complain that the famous mission building in *The Alamo* featured an anachronistic rounded top (the round part was constructed by the United States Army in 1849, some 13 years after the famous siege depicted in the film), or that the site of the *Gunfight at the O.K. Corral* was geographically inaccurate (Earp, Holliday and the others actually did battle a few buildings farther down the street). What matters more than these slight deviations from the record is the sentiment, the mythos the filmmakers successfully impart. While the storylines concentrate on ranching and farming, gunfighting, and clashes between cultures — all an indisputable part of America's westward growth — the thematic emphasis is on the importance of friendship and family.

1

It is not my intention to disparage other films by omitting them here. The 14 Westerns in this book were chosen as particularly outstanding and revealing examples from among their kind. And yes, they are personal favorites of mine; but they are also beloved across the country and across generations, which suggests that they represent something in the national character to which American audiences intuitively respond.

John Ford, John Wayne, Sam Peckinpah and Clint Eastwood are but a few of the filmmakers in the Western genre whose work has withstood the test of time. Like actual figures of the nineteenth-century West — men like Davy Crockett, Jim Bowie, Wyatt Earp and Doc Holliday — these filmmakers may become more legendary in the next century. Their nostalgic veneration of the Western experience, which helped raise their films to the status of classics, will help insure their continued fame.

From John Wayne's Ringo Kid in *Stagecoach* to Clint Eastwood's William Munny in *Unforgiven*, the Western film hero, both fictional and nonfictional, is given free rein in these films. Surely a slow demythologizing of the hero was taking place in the 53 years between Ringo and Munny, yet both characters are seen in a common pursuit, risking their lives in a grim quest to avenge the killings of those they loved. Their kind of vengeance is against the law, yet it follows the code of frontier justice. It is likely that Americans will always have a fascination for this code and those bound by it. This fascination, in turn, insures a continued audience for films that explore the mythos of the Old West and the evolution of its heroes.

You may need me and this Winchester, Curley.
I saw a ranch house burnin' last night.

JOHN WAYNE *as the Ringo Kid*

Stagecoach

1939

John Ford makes good use of the scenery of his beloved Monument Valley in this
scene from *Stagecoach*.

STAGECOACH

A Walter Wanger Presentation. Released by United Artists, 1939. Warner Home Video. 97 minutes.

Credits: John Ford (Director); Walter Wanger (Producer); Wingate Smith (Assistant Director); Yakima Canutt (Second Unit Director); Dudley Nichols (Screenplay); Bert Glennon (Photographer); Otho Lovering, Dorothy Spencer (Editors); Alexander Toluboff (Art Director); Wiard B. Ihnen (Associate Art Director); Walter Plunkett (Costumes); Ray Binger (Special Effects); Richard Hageman, Franke Harling, Louis Gruenberg, John Leipold, Leo Shuken (Music Score — adapted from American folk songs); Boris Morros (Music Direction). Based on the short story *Stage to Lordsburg* by Ernest Haycox.

Cast: Claire Trevor (Dallas); John Wayne (The Ringo Kid); Andy Devine (Buck); John Carradine (Hatfield); Thomas Mitchell (Doc Boone); Louise Platt (Lucy Mallory); George Bancroft (Curley); Donald Meek (Peacock); Berton Churchill (Gatewood); Tim Holt (Lieutenant); Tom Tyler (Luke Plummer); Joseph Rickson (Hank Plummer); Vester Pegg (Ike Plummer); Chris Pin Martin (Chris); Elvira Rios (Yakima, His Wife); Francis Ford (Billy Pickett); Kent Odell (Billy Pickett, Jr.); Marga Daighton (Mrs. Pickett); Harry Tenbrook (Telegraph Operator); Jack Pennick (Jerry, the Bartender); Paul McVey (Express Agent); Cornelius Keefe (Capt. Whitney); Florence Lake (Mrs. Whitney); Louis Mason (Sheriff); Brenda Fowler (Mrs. Gatewood); Walter McGrail (Capt. Sickel); William Hoffer (Sergeant); Bryant Washburn (Capt. Simmons); Nora Cecil (Doc Boone's Housekeeper); Chief White Horse (Indian Chief); Duke Lee (Sheriff of Lordsburg); Mary Kathleen Walker (Lucy's Baby); Helen Gibson, Dorothy Appleby (Saloon Girls); Buddy Roosevelt, Bill Cody (Ranchers). Also Ed Brady, Steve Clemente, Theodore Lorch, Fritzi Brunette, Leonard Trainor, Chris Phillips, Tex Driscoll, Teddy Billings, John Eckert, Al Lee, Jack Mohr, Patsy Doyle, Wiggie Blowne, Margaret Smith, Yakima Canutt.

Synopsis

In the 1880s, trouble breaks out between the Apache Indians and the white pioneers out West. The Apache leader Geronimo has left the reservation and is on the warpath.

An Overland Line stagecoach arrives in Tonto, Arizona, en route to its destination in Lordsburg, New Mexico. Buck, the stagecoach driver, would rather not venture on because of the Indian danger, but a cavalry detachment will travel along. Tonto's marshal, Curley, decides to ride shotgun after learning the Ringo Kid has escaped from prison. The accompanying cavalry unit will be met by another patrol at the first stop at Dry Fork. Passenger Lucy Mallory is going to Dry Fork to meet her husband, an officer in the army. She is pregnant. A gambler and gunfighter named Hatfield, who had known Mrs. Mallory's father during the Civil War, offers her his protection on the stagecoach ride. A jittery whiskey salesman, Mr. Peacock, is coerced into making the journey by fellow passenger Doc Boone, whose drinking problem is exacerbated by the man's ample supply of samples. The good doctor and a prostitute named Dallas are being escorted out of town by the priggish ladies of the Law and Order League.

Leaving Tonto, the stagecoach picks up the town banker, Gatewood, who has secretly extorted the bank's funds. Out in the desert, the Ringo Kid stops the stage and climbs aboard. Ringo has broken out of jail to avenge the murders of his father and brother at the hands of the Plummer brothers. The Kid was put in jail on a dubious charge of killing the Plummers' foreman. Both Buck and Curley are sympathetic to Ringo, but the marshal takes away his rifle and arrests him.

The cavalry unit can only stay with the stagecoach to the first relay station, but the second patrol is delayed due to the Indian trouble. All aboard the stage vote whether to go on or not, and the decision is to travel on. Hatfield and Mrs. Mallory snub Dallas, but Doc Boone and Ringo treat her with kindness. Gatewood is rude to everyone.

At the second station, Apache Wells, Mrs. Mallory learns that her husband was hurt in a fight between the cavalry and the Indians. This tragic news and her pregnancy cause her to collapse. Doc Boone, realizing she is about to give birth, forces himself out of his drunken stupor to deliver the baby. With Dallas' help, the doctor is brilliant and both mother and child pull through. Upon seeing the tender feelings that Dallas has for the baby and its mother, Ringo reveals his own by asking her to marry him. Although taken aback, she realizes that she cares for him as well. Dallas then tries to help the Kid to escape, but he doesn't go after spotting Indian smoke signals which signal an impending attack.

The Apaches attack the stagecoach during its frantic race to Lordsburg, and Peacock is wounded. Curley gives Ringo his rifle and the Kid turns it with deadly accuracy on the pursuing Indians. At one point, after Buck is also wounded and has lost the reins, Ringo jumps onto the stage's horses to retrieve them. The Indians are all around the coach, and Hatfield prepares to shoot Lucy to keep her from capture and torture. They hear a bugle and the cavalry arrives just in time to save all in the coach except the gambler, who is mortally wounded by the Apaches. As he dies, the soldiers drive away the attacking Indians.

Left to right, standing: Andy Devine, George Bancroft, Tim Holt, John Carradine. *Seated:* John Wayne, Claire Trevor, Louise Platt, Francis Ford, Thomas Mitchell. *Partially obscured:* Berton Churchill.

In Lordsburg, Gatewood is arrested and Lucy thanks Dallas for her help. Doc is able to keep Luke Plummer from using a shotgun against Ringo. Confronting the three murderous brothers in the middle of the street, the Kid kills them all. Curley then changes his mind about arresting him and, with Doc's assistance, sends Ringo and Dallas over the border for a new life together.

Many people have thought of the Old West as a legendary environment that existed in the era just following the Civil War — the 1860s to the 1880s — yet it existed long before this conflict and into the twentieth century. In the earliest years of the West, mountain men, trappers and pathfinders opened up new trails for emigrant families who dared to hope for better lives. These pioneers became ranchers, farmers and townsfolk, and brought progress and change to the Western wilderness. The railroad brought settlers to the West by the thousands whereas the covered wagon had brought only the hardiest. The cowboy was born out of this change and so was the outlaw. The advancing civilization believed in conquering the frontier. The Indians, the first Westerners, were forced to fight for their lands and heritage. But fighting was done by many different groups of people because there was a resolve to use force if necessary to gain anything that was wanted and needed. This resolution, whether right or wrong, was the American way. The West was America's own gain, nurtured by the progress and change; yet America lost some of what was grand about the West in the very process of conquering it.

Western films have been around since Thomas Edison invented the motion picture camera in the late nineteenth century. Interest in stories of the Old West began as well during that century, notably in the dime novels written by Ned Buntline about William "Buffalo Bill" Cody. So popular did Cody's legend become as a result of these action-packed yet exaggerated adventures that he created a spectacular Wild West Show; Buffalo Bill, in fact, appeared in early silent newsreels. In 1903, a ten-minute film from the Edison Company, *The Great Train Robbery* (Edwin S. Porter, director), established the Western as a recognizable storyline. Just a year earlier, Owen Wister had written the Western novel *The Virginian*, which gave serious credence to the lone cowboy as a strong, heroic figure. An actor named G.M. Anderson, who had a small part in *The Great Train Robbery*, became the first cowboy hero in silent pictures; acting under the name Broncho Billy Anderson, he took a film company to California and made hundreds of films between 1908 and 1916. The film capital Hollywood was born during these years, and other film makers who soon contributed to the Western genre included Cecil B. DeMille, D.W. Griffith and Thomas Ince. It was Ince who introduced the second great cowboy star, William S. Hart, to audiences in 1914. For the following 12 years, Hart made "A" Westerns which were strong on characterization, story, realism and romanticism. Tom Mix actually appeared in films before Hart, starting in 1909, and by 1917 had made his mark on the Western. Mix was a showman, as was Buffalo Bill, and his colorful costumes, simple plots and plentiful action scenes fostered the "B" Western, geared mainly for children, and created by Broncho Billy. There were many imitators who followed and had their own popularity. Two of the most famous stars of the sound era were the singing cowboys Gene Autry and Roy Rogers, establishing themselves in the 1930s.

Westerns had declined in popularity by the end of silent pictures — the self-righteous cowboys portrayed on the screen by an array of stars remained children's heroes, but lost their edge with adult audiences. With the advent of sound in films, Westerns were not immediately looked upon with favor by the major studios. The Poverty Row Studios continued to churn out their low budgeted "B" Westerns, but the "A" Western suffered. Exceptions included the first sound Western, *In Old Arizona* (Raoul Walsh, director); its star, Warner Baxter, won an Academy Award for Best Actor with his dashing performance as the Cisco Kid. RKO's 1931 epic *Cimarron* (Wesley Ruggles, director) was the first Western to win the Oscar for Best Picture. The occasional epics had lent prestige to the Western genre since Paramount's 1923 silent *The Covered Wagon* (James Cruze, director). But the "B" Westerns dominated in the 1930s as they did in the silent years. Even a big studio like Paramount profited immensely with its series of "B" grade Hopalong Cassidy films starring William Boyd — in fact, their success inspired the studio to renew their interest in "A" Westerns. Many big studios followed with quality Westerns and the boom year was 1939. Among the top Westerns that year were Warner Bros.' *Dodge City* (Michael Curtiz, director), 20th Century–Fox's *Jesse James* (Henry King, director), and, most significantly, *Stagecoach*.

Called the renaissance Western, *Stagecoach* was recognized as the film which rescued the mainstream Western from the childlike confines of the "B" scenario. Although there were distinguished and respectable "A" Westerns before *Stagecoach*, its perfect blend of characterization, action and poetic images rewarded the film with especial distinction; it stimulated the genre's standing as a serious art form, and its respectability was reinforced. The lion's share of the credit must go to its director, John Ford. This was Ford's first sound Western, but he was no stranger to silent Westerns — his last one prior to *Stagecoach* was Fox's *Three Bad Men* (1926). Two years earlier, he also directed for Fox the great Western epic *The Iron Horse*.

Ford first came to Hollywood in 1914, following his brother Frances, who was already established in films, and eventually he became a director at Universal. Among his first directorial assignments were Westerns — a two-reeler called *The Soul Herder* and the feature *Straight Shooting*. Both were made in 1917 and starred Harry Carey. Ford showcased Carey as a realistic yet sentimental Westerner named Cheyenne Harry, and they made 26 Westerns together. Moving on to Fox, Ford directed Westerns for cowboy stars Tom Mix and Buck Jones. Early in his career Ford developed the Western theme of people making better lives for themselves in a wild frontier; he liked filming in the wide, open spaces.

Ford left Fox in 1931, worked at various studios and earned his first Oscar for RKO's *The Informer* (1935), about a man who betrays a comrade and is troubled by the retribution. Ford was interested in stories about outcasts of society who somehow ennobled themselves after great adversity. In 1937, he bought for $2500 the film rights to Ernest Haycox's short story *Stage to Lordsburg*, whose hero is a gunman and heroine a prostitute. Dudley Nichols, who won an Oscar for his screenplay on *The Informer,* was given the task of writing a scenario from Haycox's story. Ford, who worked with Nichols, was also inspired by the Western stories of Bret Harte, notably *The Outcasts of Poker Flat,* which was the first to let the hero treat a prostitute with respect. Another inspiration came from Guy de Maupassant's French story *Boule de Suif,* which has a prostitute giving herself to an enemy officer during the Franco-Prussian War to safeguard a coach full of hateful passengers.

For the screenplay, Haycox's basic storyline (a stagecoach journeying from Tonto to Lordsburg during Apache upheaval) was retained but all the characters' names were changed. For example, Malpais Bill became the Ringo Kid and Henriette became Dallas; some of these characters had names similar to those in Stuart N. Lake's book, *Wyatt Earp: Frontier Marshal.* The main difference between the short story and screenplay is the bringing together of hero and heroine. The whiskey drummer dies in Haycox's piece due to the stress of the coach ride; Henriette comforts him in her arms and this kindness attracts Malpais Bill to her. In the screenplay, Ringo is especially attracted to Dallas when she reveals her own maternal instincts with Lucy Mallory's baby. However, the suspenseful endings are intact—after the thrill of the Indian chase, Malpais Bill and Ringo leave the sides of their ladies to shoot it out with their enemies. In the film the actual gunplay is not visualized except for Ringo dropping into the dirt with his rifle blazing.

Ford took the script to the biggest studios—Columbia, MGM, Paramount, Warner Bros.—and they rejected it as uncommercial because they believed Westerns were out-of-date. Merian C. Cooper, vice-president of Selznick International, an independent company headed by David O. Selznick, signed Ford to direct the film as a big Technicolor presentation. Selznick wanted Gary Cooper and Marlene Dietrich for the hero and heroine. But Ford already had made a verbal agreement with John Wayne and Claire Trevor and this caused a conflict with Selznick which ended their deal. Ford then interested another independent producer, Walter Wanger, in the project. Wanger also wanted Gary Cooper, who at the time was a bigger star than Duke Wayne, but relented when Ford agreed to do the picture on a smaller budget and in black-and-white.

Nicknamed Duke because of his childhood affection for a pet dog, John Wayne first became involved in films as a grip, carrying props and sweeping up in the late 1920s at Fox. Legend has it that he swept himself onto a set with director Ford, who used him as an extra in a few films and even helped him get the starring role in 1930's Western epic for Fox, *The Big Trail* (Raoul Walsh, director). That picture was not a big success, and Wayne was relegated to making "B" Westerns for other studios during the decade, most famously as one of the Three Mesquiteers in a series of films for Republic Pictures.

By the time of *Stagecoach*, Ford felt Duke Wayne had developed a strength, physical grace and vulnerability that would appeal to all audiences. They were also good friends. According to an oft-told story, Ford approached Duke for the role of Ringo, but asked first who he thought could play the part. The actor mentioned Lloyd Nolan. But Ford believed Wayne was a perfect choice and certainly went against all obstacles to have him in the picture, including having to convince Herbert Yates, head of Republic and Wayne's boss, for the loanout. Yet, once filming began in 1938, Ford was relentless in badgering Duke in front of cast and crew; the reasons were to make the more distinguished performers in the cast not feel intimidated by having a less reputed actor in a starring role, and to make Wayne reach inside himself for a better performance. The ploys worked as John Ford had the whole cast sympathizing with Duke, and he gave a topnotch performance. All the charismatic traits foreseen by Ford were nobly displayed. So pleased was he with Wayne's performance that he reshot the actor's legendary opening scene as Ringo stands tall in the desert, twirling his Winchester rifle and calling a halt to the stage.

All the characters in the film were more richly defined than those in the short story and this was a classic development enhancing the maturity of Westerns. Both strengths and weaknesses were revealed in each character. The Ringo Kid is an outlaw only because of an injustice, and Dallas is a prostitute because she had to fend for herself, having lost her parents at an early age. The poignancy is overwhelming in the tender moments when Ringo follows Dallas through the shadows of a picturesque evening, or when he escorts her home and finds his love has not diminished upon learning of her profession. John Wayne's youthful innocence, his complete lack of social prejudice, is beautifully realized. Claire Trevor's Dallas truly has a heart of gold.

At the heart of this movie are its three most controversial characters — the prostitute, the outlaw, the drunken doctor — who end up being the most noble of the bunch. Thomas Mitchell earned an Academy Award for Best Supporting Actor for his performance as lovable Doc Boone, who shows great courage not only helping a pregnant Lucy Mallory but in risking his life for Ringo against Luke Plummer. Louise Platt was a contract player for Walter Wanger; Platt's Lucy, while prim and proper, is snobbish until she learns lessons in humility and gratitude from both Doc and Dallas.

Mitchell and the other male supporting actors had all worked for John Ford on previous films. John Carradine's mysterious gambler Hatfield secretly comes from a Southern aristocracy; his gallantry towards Lucy is a reflection of this and her own Southern roots. Donald Meek's whiskey drummer is the gentle buffer upon which the comic but sad figure of Doc is allowed to play off of, yet he is also firm in reminding the other men to be quiet after the birth of Lucy's baby. The most faulty character is the corrupt banker (Berton

Churchill) who hides behind his obnoxious pomposity; his only extenuating circumstance is having a somewhat shrewish wife capable of driving any man to desperate measures. Andy Devine's Buck, the stage driver, is treated as something of a lout, but he is a professional weathering many obstacles in his handling of the coach.

George Bancroft as Curley, the wise and stalwart marshal, may be the film's strongest character. The Kid seeks vengeance against the Plummers and Curley, acting as a concerned father figure, understands this need for frontier justice. Doc Boone is the father figure for Dallas. It is a wonderful moment when both Doc and Curley allow Ringo and Dallas to realize their love; the decent human emotions laid bare in the film's last scene seemed to outweigh any questions of right or wrong a viewer might have about the Kid. The entire cast was memorable.

Probably the most memorable things about *Stagecoach* were the action scenes and the emergence of Duke Wayne as a top Hollywood star. In the 1932 serial *Shadow of the Eagle* (Ford Beebe, director), Wayne was doubled by stuntman Yakima Canutt. Among other things, Canutt had been a real rodeo star and even a cowboy actor in a series of silent "B" Westerns for independent producer Ben Wilson. Other "B" pictures followed for Canutt, who doubled again for Duke and others until introduced to John Ford. As a renowned stuntman, Yakima was assigned to second unit director chores on *Stagecoach*, coordinating all the physical action. The first scene Canutt worked on was the stage's river crossing; a log is strapped to each side of the coach to help it stay afloat and an onshore pulley (not seen in the picture) was attached to an underwater cable to assist the vehicle. The scene was shot on the Kern River near Kernville, California. But Canutt's famous work was seen in the breathtaking Indian chase (the last scene filmed), shot on Muroc Dry Lake near Victorville, California.

Many of the horse falls here were accomplished using "Running W's"— the horse's legs were secured to a long cable in the ground, and when the cable ran out, the animal toppled over. Yakima stunted once again for Wayne when the Ringo Kid leaps onto the team of six horses from the coach to pick up the fallen reins. Canutt created the amazing stunt where a rider falls beneath a team of horses, grabs onto the coach as it passes over, then climbs up the rear of the coach. (This stunt was first used in 1937 for Monogram's *Riders of the Dawn*; R.N. Bradbury, director). A variant of this is used in *Stagecoach*, as Yakima, playing an Indian, jumps onto the team of horses from his own mount, is shot by Ringo and falls under the horses and coach. Ford was overwhelmed by this incredible deed, stating that even had there been no film in the camera it would not have been shot over. The director was chided for the chase, particularly by William S. Hart, who claimed the Indians would have ended it immediately by shooting the coach's horses. Ford responded with, "If they had, it would have been the end of the picture, wouldn't it?"

Several of the sweeping background scenes were filmed in Monument Valley, 2,000 square miles of desert, buttes and mesas on the Utah-Arizona border. So powerful is the presence of the Valley that it is widely thought to have played a far larger role in the film. It was Ford's first use of Monument Valley.

While the Indians in *Stagecoach* are portrayed as one dimensional savage forces, the Navajo Indians living in the Valley were treated well by Ford, becoming part of this and many future films at this location. They were extremely poor, living under primitive conditions, and Ford helped them get jobs on the film as extras and laborers. Republic Pictures' Western town was used for Tonto, while the Goldwyn lot was used for Lordsburg and all other interiors. For the close-ups of the principals inside the coach, a mock-up on rollers was used with rear projection footage. An actual Concord stagecoach was used for the outdoor locations.

In the early 1850s, stages were used in California to serve the mining interests; among the first were from Wells Fargo and the California Stage Company. John Butterfield's Overland Mail Co. followed in 1857, and soon coaches ran over 2,800 miles from Missouri to California. These arduous journeys were true tests of endurance for all. In 1861, Ben Holladay and Wells Fargo both bought out separate aspects of Butterfield's company. In 1866 Holladay sold his interests totally to Wells Fargo.

In 1936, Walter Wanger produced for Paramount *The Trail of the Lonesome Pine* (Henry Hathaway, director). The first outdoor film in Technicolor, it was brought in under budget by Wanger. In 1938 United Artists entrusted Wanger with $2,000,000 to produce a series of films, but Wanger initially was not frugal enough and lost money for the studio. However, three Wanger properties would earn money for UA, and one of those was *Stagecoach*.

Made on a budget of $392,000, the picture grossed $1,000,000 domestically within a year of its March 1939 release. Not the biggest box office Western of the year, that distinction was shared by *Jesse James* and John Ford's *Drums Along the Mohawk* (Ford's Technicolor entry was also more expensive to produce.) But *Stagecoach* was clearly the most prestigious. The New York Film Critics voted Ford their award for Best Direction.

The Motion Picture Academy of Arts and Sciences nominated Ford for an Oscar as Best Director and the film as Best Picture — as well as bestowing nominations on Mitchell, Bert Glennon for Cinematography (Black-and-White), Alexander Toluboff for Interior Decoration, Otho Lovering and Dorothy Spencer for Film Editing, and Best Score. The Western won two Academy Awards, for its Score as well as Supporting Actor. The music award — shared by Richard Hageman, Franke Harling, Louis Gruenberg, John Leipold and Leo Shuken — was for a compilation of beloved American folk tunes. "Bury Me Not on the Lone Prairie" is the stagecoach theme.

Nineteen hundred thirty-nine was the year of David Selznick and MGM's epic drama of the Old South, *Gone with the Wind* — it won, among its Oscars, Best Picture, Director (Victor Fleming), Interior Decoration and Editing. The Oscar for Black-and-White Cinematography went to Gregg Toland for United Artists' *Wuthering Heights* (William Wyler, director).

Although there are moments in *Stagecoach* which seem like clichés by now — the cavalry coming to the rescue in the nick of time is a prime example — in 1939, the film was innovative and daring. There were two inferior remakes — a 1966 version for 20th Century–Fox (Gordon Douglas, director), and in 1986 for CBS Television (Ted Post, director).

But the original is given the credit for sustaining the tradition of adult Westerns with its scope and its approach. The narrative takes time to give the characters depth and presence; while they seem to fit in perhaps too theatrically, they are a part of the time and place that is given a direct foundation in an American past. Ford believed in authenticity, but even more he believed in the frontier spirit that certainly mythologized the Old West.

A thunderous Indian chase, the visual splendor of Monument Valley, a hero with the aura of a knight — these may or may not have been part of a real West. Ford, no doubt, loved to think so. *Stagecoach* is important because it has made us believe and feel Ford's dream as well. It sustained the great poetic images we all wish to share, and it doesn't matter that it might be simply myth because our dreams are more valuable than what might have really been. The John Ford Westerns made in the next quarter century, often with Duke Wayne and a loyal stock company of both cast and crew, are a warm and deeply personal expression of an American heritage.

Reviews

Newsweek: "Against the pictorially thrilling Arizona background, the action of *Stagecoach* builds from its initial suspense into a steady crescendo of excitement. The acting is uniformly excellent."

The New York Times: "They've all done nobly by a noble horse opera, but none so nobly as its director. This is one stagecoach that's powered by a Ford."

*There'll be no quittin' along the way. Not by me
and not by you.*

JOHN WAYNE *as Tom Dunson, to his cowboys*

Red River

1948

Walter Brennan (right) makes his point to John Wayne, as Montgomery Clift (center) looks on.

RED RIVER

A Monterey Production. Released by United Artists, 1948.
MGM/UA Home Video. 134 minutes.

Credits: Howard Hawks (Director and Producer); Charles K. Feldman (Executive Producer); Arthur Rosson (Co-director); William McGarry (Assistant Director); Borden Chase, Charles Schnee (Screenplay); Russell Harlan (Photographer); Christian Nyby (Editor); John Datu Arensma (Art Director); Lee Greenway (Makeup); Donald Steward (Special Effects); Allan Thompson (Special Photographic Effects); Dimitri Tiomkin (Music Score). Song: "Settle Down" by Dimitri Tiomkin. Based on the *Saturday Evening Post* story *The Chisholm Trail* by Borden Chase.

Cast: John Wayne (Thomas Dunson); Montgomery Clift (Matthew Garth); Joanne Dru (Tess Millay); Walter Brennan (Groot Nadine); Coleen Gray (Fen); Harry Carey, Sr. (Mr. Melville); John Ireland (Cherry Valance); Noah Beery, Jr. (Buster McGee); Harry Carey, Jr. (Dan Latimer); Chief Yowlachie (Quo); Paul Fix (Teeler Yacey); Hank Worden (Simms); Mickey Kuhn (Matthew, as a Boy); Ray Hyke (Walt Jergens); Hal Taliaferro (Old Leather); Ivan Parry (Bunk Kenneally); Paul Fierro (Fernandez); Billy Self (Wounded Wrangler); Tom Tyler (Quitter); Lane Chandler (Colonel); Glenn Strange (Naylor); Shelley Winters (Dance Hall Girl); Dan White (Laredo).

Synopsis

In 1851, Tom Dunson and Groot Nadine are on a wagon train bound for California. They had not officially signed on but had joined the train on the trail outside of St. Louis. With a desire to go South to Texas and start a cattle ranch, Tom, accompanied by Groot, leaves the wagon train. Tom will not let Fen, the woman he loves, go with them despite her pleas, but he promises to send for her later on.

Hours later, Tom and Groot see smoke coming from the direction of the wagons and realize there has been an Indian attack. A few Indians attack the two men, but are killed. One of the dead braves is wearing the bracelet Tom gave to Fen. A boy named Matthew Garth, a survivor of the raid, joins Groot and Tom. The three journey across the Red River and into Texas until Tom finds the land he wants. With his bull and the boy's cow, Tom begins his cattle ranch with a brand called the Red River D; he assures Matt that someday his own name will be added if he earns it. Two strangers approach the trio, warning them they are trespassing; Tom knows the land belongs to the strongest and decides to fight for it. In 14 years, with fighting and hard work, Tom Dunson builds up a massive cattle empire.

Matt Garth, Tom's foster son, now wears the bracelet. Recently returned from the Civil War, Matt agrees to help Tom take the huge herd of cattle to Missouri (the beef market has collapsed in Texas due to the war). Ten thousand head of cattle have been rounded up and branded for the 1,000-mile drive; among the cowboys are Cherry Valance, Buster McGee, Dan Latimer and Bunk Kenneally. Tom tells the men that once they sign on, they cannot quit. Groot runs the chuck wagon.

During the drive, Cherry suggests going to Abilene, Kansas, a possible cattle market, but Tom is against this. A stubborn and hard man, the drive makes him harder for his whole life is tied up in it. When Bunk makes a ruckus one night stealing sugar from the chuck wagon, a stampede breaks out and Dan is killed. Tom tries to whip Bunk as punishment, only the younger man refuses to be beaten; Tom appears ready to gun him down, but Matt steps in, wounding Bunk instead. Some cattle and supplies have been lost in the stampede and the men do not like the new short rations.

The cowboys come across a wrangler from another cattle outfit, survivor of an ambush by border bandits; he urges them to avoid the outlaws by taking the safer trail to Abilene. Tom is against it. When three of his cowboys try to quit, Tom, Matt and Cherry are forced to shoot them. Three more men sneak off in the night. After the herd is taken across the Red River, Cherry returns with two of the men, having had to shoot one on the trail. Half-crazed from drink and lack of sleep, Tom tells the two deserters they will be hanged, but Matt, Cherry and Buster stop him. Matt takes the cattle away from him and leaves Tom behind, taking the herd to Abilene. Tom vows to kill Matt even though he is told he will benefit the most from the Abilene sale.

The cowboys are haunted by the fear that Tom will follow; later on, they save a wagon train being attacked by Indians. Tess Millay is one of the passengers and she and Matt fall in love. She realizes that Matt also cares for Tom. With a band of gunmen, Tom does follow Matt's trail, but he first meets Tess, who explains how she was left behind like Tom had left Fen. Tom is still set on killing Matt; Tess offers to bear a son for Tom to save Matt's life (thus filling Dunson's pain at the loss of his foster son). Tom refuses to give up his grim quest, but he does allow Tess to go to Abilene with him.

In Abilene, businessman Mr. Melville buys the entire herd from Matt and the other cowboys at 21 dollars a head. An enormous check is approved by Matt to be given to Tom. That night, Tess warns Matt that Tom is just outside town and gunning for him.

The next morning, Tom rides into town and is wounded by Cherry, who is shot as well. Tom confronts Matt, but Matt will not draw his gun despite

Cattle crossing the Red River.

Tom's badgering. There is a brutal fistfight until Tess stops it at gunpoint, making the two realize they love each other like father and son. Tom tells Matt that from now on their Red River brand will carry his name, too, because he has earned it.

The great revival of Western films, begun in 1939 with *Stagecoach*, continued when the United States entered the Second World War in 1941. Westerns were a testament to the country's history, although romanticized more times than not, and American values and pride were strengthened because of the war. Like this conflict, the Western genre symbolized the fight for freedom through sacrifice and sustained the belief in a better way of life.

During the 1940s, the "B" Western format continued to prosper and even had their heroes battling Nazis and other assorted bad guys in modern settings. The three most popular "B" cowboys were Roy Rogers, Gene Autry and

William Boyd. The "A" Westerns in the early years of the decade included historical epics like MGM's *Northwest Passage* (1940; King Vidor, director), and Warner Bros.' *They Died with Their Boots On* (1941; Raoul Walsh, director). After the glamorization of the outlaw in 1939's *Jesse James*, other films profiled "noble" badmen, including a *Jesse James* sequel in '40 called *The Return of Frank James* (Fritz Lang, director; with Henry Fonda reprising his role as Jesse's brother). MGM offered a 1941 version of *Billy the Kid* (David Miller, director), the first Western shot in color in Monument Valley.

With the war years came a further maturity to Westerns. Some featured social issues (for example, 20th Century–Fox's *The Ox-Bow Incident,* 1943; William Wellman, director) or sex (David Selznick's sprawling 1946 epic, *Duel in the Sun*; King Vidor, director). Then there was the psychological Western such as Warner Bros.' 1947 feature, *Pursued* (Raoul Walsh, director), where the hero is haunted by a past trauma. John Ford directed several great Westerns during the decade — notably 20th Century–Fox's *My Darling Clementine* (1946) and RKO's *She Wore a Yellow Ribbon* ('49). The year 1948 was an exceptional one for Western films, particularly with Warner Bros.' *The Treasure of the Sierra Madre* (John Huston, director), and *Red River*. Huston's picture (about greed) and *The Ox-Bow Incident* (about lynch law) were the only Western films to receive Academy Award nominations for Best Picture in the 1940s. It should be mentioned that *The Treasure of the Sierra Madre* and earlier films like *Northwest Passage, Drums Along the Mohawk* and *The Trail of the Lonesome Pine,* are not true Westerns in time and place but are in look and feel.

The epic Western was given a sure-fire shot in the arm with *Red River*. While some epics of the 1940s were quite spectacular, they seemed to meander along, trying to cover too many things. Director-producer Howard Hawks endowed his Western with moments of spectacle, but forged the story around just one thing, the relationship between father and son. This is such powerful drama that it outweighs the controversial glossy ending. The film has the distinction of being the finest Western about a cattle drive. Hawks was so proud of it he boasted to his friend and colleague John Ford that it was nearly as good a Western as anything Ford could make.

Howard Hawks, like Ford, started in the movie business during the silent years — in 1916 he was with the property department at the Famous Players-Lasky Studio. Ten years later, after spending a good deal of time writing scripts, Hawks directed his first feature film, *The Road to Glory*. (He had directed scenes in a 1917 silent as well as a few comedy shorts.) While *Red River* is credited as director Hawks' first Western, he did do uncredited work on two earlier ones, MGM's *Viva Villa* in 1934, and Howard Hughes' *The Outlaw* in 1940. The latter film was finally released in 1943, after surmounting some censorship problems created by its sexual overtones; Hughes took the director's credit.

Jack Conway received credit for the direction of *Viva Villa*; Hawks, who assisted Ben Hecht on the script, went uncredited on the screenplay as well. Incidentally, *Viva Villa* was Oscar-nominated for Best Picture and Writing (Adaptation). Like John Ford, Hawks enjoyed making Westerns out in the open air away from the confines of the studio, but unlike Ford, who made 15 sound Westerns (and a few dozen silent ones), he directed only five. Hawks' finest films in the 1940s were Warner Bros.' *Sergeant York*, a 1941 war drama on the life of Alvin C. York (he was nominated for an Academy Award as Best Director) and *Red River*.

The screen rights to the Borden Chase story *The Chisholm Trail* were bought by Hawks before it was even serialized by *The Saturday Evening Post* in six installments between December 1946 and January 1947. In fact, the film was shot in '46 between June and November. Hawks set up his own independent company, Monterey Productions, to produce the picture for distribution by United Artists. Chase and later Charles Schnee were hired to write the screenplay; uncredited writers included Leigh Brackett and Jules Furthman.

Chase's original story featured many incidents that did not find their way into the film. In the story's first stampede (there are three), three cowboys are trampled to death, not just the one cowboy in the movie's single stampede. In the story Tess Millay is a cafe singer whom Matthew Garth had met in Memphis before the cattle drive, and she becomes involved with a gambler named Clark Donegal; in the film she meets Matt late in the drive and there is no involvement with any Donegal, except for a mention that he runs the wagon train of gamblers she is on. During the cattle crossing of the Red River in the story, three cowboys drown; the film depicts a calm crossing and the tired men getting the herd across. Cherry Valance kills Donegal over Tess in Chase's story, and he even tries to steal the herd; the movie has Cherry staying with Matt and the cattle into Abilene, where he is wounded by Tom Dunson. Tess is also involved with Dunson in Chase's story but, as in the film, she loves Matthew.

The most significant difference between story and film is the ending. Chase has Dunson shooting Matthew in the arm before collapsing from loss of blood and a damaged lung (caused by Cherry's earlier bullet). Dunson is then taken in a wagon by Matthew and Tess back across the Red River to Texas where he dies and is buried beside the river. As Ford often did in his Westerns, Hawks revealed that he could be a sentimentalist by letting Tom live and reconcile with his foster son, but only after a savage fistfight. Chase disapproved of the changes, particularly the ending, but Howard Hawks apparently could not bear to kill off Tom Dunson because he liked the character too much and he felt the ending worked better this way.

Gary Cooper was originally asked to portray Dunson, but he wanted no part of the character's ruthlessness; Cary Grant declined the supporting part of Cherry. Hawks planned to have his discovery Margaret Sheridan play Tess, but she became pregnant and had to drop out of the picture. Joanne Dru's role was then changed somewhat because Tess was initially going to be a gambling lady who could do fancy card tricks.

Duke Wayne had doubts he could play Dunson because, at 41, he was younger than this character, but Hawks gave him the necessary reassurance. He was an established star by this stage in his film career and had made some mighty fine Westerns between *Stagecoach* and *Red River*— Republic's *Dark Command* (1940; Raoul Walsh, director), RKO's *Tall in the Saddle* (1944; Edwin L. Marin, director) and, the same year as Hawks' Western, two for John Ford, RKO's *Fort Apache* and MGM's *Three Godfathers*. After seeing him in *Red River*, Ford quipped that he didn't realize Wayne could act. Indeed, his powerful performance as the tough, hardheaded cattle baron is one of his most memorable, and his best at the time. Ford was so impressed with Wayne's portrayal of an older man that he gave him the opportunity to play one in *She Wore a Yellow Ribbon*, thus creating another memorable performance.

In 1945, Montgomery Clift was starring in a Broadway play called *You Touched Me!* (Guthrie McClintic, producer and director). Howard Hawks was impressed with Clift's performance in the stage drama and offered him the role of Matthew in *Red River*. The young actor had been performing in the theater since 1933 when he was 13 years old. Before the Hawks offer, Clift made an unsuccessful screen test for another Western, *Pursued*. Although he expressed doubts about playing a cowboy, Montgomery was taught how to ride a horse through difficult Western terrain, and he also mastered the fast draw and the cowboy's gait. He held his own with Duke Wayne and gave a strong performance, although Clift felt it was a "mediocre" one. Established was the gentle strength that would serve Montgomery so well in later pictures. Although *Red River* was his first film, it was not released until after MGM's 1948 drama, *The Search* (Fred Zinnemann, director). For this second film, Montgomery earned an Oscar nomination for Best Actor.

Wayne and Clift shared a high regard for each other's acting in the Western. In the scene where Tom confronts the two deserters, Clift wanted to match his toughness, but Hawks told him to underplay and silently follow his every move instead. Duke commented to the director his admiration for Montgomery in this sequence. Clift was sure he would dominate Wayne in the scene where Matt is forced to take over command from Tom; for this scene, Hawks told Wayne to look away from Clift and quietly say he was going to kill him. Now it was Montgomery's turn to express admiration for Duke. Dunson's ruthless domination has drawn all sympathy away from him, and Matt proves the more able trail boss by bringing sympathy and understanding to his leadership. But once Tom's vulnerability is made evident, and he stands alone and lost, sympathy for him returns.

Montgomery Clift thought the ending was a "farce," and, it's true, Chase's concept of Dunson dying is more in keeping with the Western spirit. One must, however, keep in mind Tom's longing for Fen (who is not in the writer's story). It is no coincidence that the film's most poignant sequences are those in which Tom and Fen bid goodbye and when Tom meets Tess, a reflection of Fen. *Red River*'s first great visual image is of Coleen Gray's spirited Fen standing alone and dignified as Tom rides away. Tess' relationship with Matt is helped right away because he comes to her rescue during an Indian attack, unlike Tom who left Fen knowing there was Indian danger. But Matt does leave Tess behind when he goes into Abilene, and fate seems to step in to allow Tom the chance for redemption. In remembrance of his lost love, Tom brings Tess to Matt and his change of heart can be detected already; why else would he bring her to a man he was about to kill? Besides, unlike Chase's Dunson, literally a "bull of a man," the screen counterpart proves, like Matt, that real strength is in the "soft" side of oneself not afraid to reveal sensitivity and fairness. The times that Tom showed these qualities, he seemed the better man; for instance, he speaks to his cowboys before the drive, telling them there are no hard feelings if anyone doesn't want to go. Later he and Matt decide to make a dead cowboy's wish come true for his wife by sending her a pair of red shoes.

John Ireland and Joanne Dru fell in love while filming and eventually married. There was a bit of controversy during the film when Borden Chase claimed Howard Hawks was jealous over Miss Dru, gave Ireland a hard time and decreased the size of his role. The director defended himself by denying any interest in the actress and referring to Ireland's carousing as the reason for rewriting his part. Nonetheless, Tess Millay and Cherry Valance are among the two performers' greatest roles.

The whole supporting cast etched equally solid performances. Harry Carey, Jr., Ivan Parry and Tom Tyler, who was Luke Plummer in *Stagecoach*, played unfortunate cowboys who didn't finish the drive. Tyler's cowhand is shot by an obsessed Dunson for being a quitter; Parry's Bunk is almost shot down by Tom after accidentally starting the stampede; and the younger Carey's Dan is perhaps the most tragic figure in the film because of his terrible death (he can only scream as the mighty herd tramples him). Harry Carey, Sr., Noah Beery, Jr., Paul Fix and Walter Brennan all worked for Hawks on earlier films. The elder Carey's honest cattle buyer is a great reminder of just what a decent figure this fine actor cut in many films. Noah's amiable personality as Buster is also warmly felt. Fix's Teeler, although a deserter, reinforces the actor's dignity as he reminds the other cowboys that they all have a stake in the herd. And Brennan's Groot Nadine is irascible yet amusing as the main comic foil, relieving the tension in the otherwise harsh tale.

One of Hollywood's most endearing character actors, Brennan also did the off-screen narration in one version of *Red River*. Another version did not use the actor's narration, instead focusing on a handwritten book called "Early Tales of Texas," shown on screen every so often to help the story along. This latter version is the restored director's cut seen on MGM/UA Home Video.

Apparently, Borden Chase and Howard Hawks took their inspiration for *Red River* from two famous sources — the 1935 film *Mutiny on the Bounty* and the King Ranch. In MGM's sea epic (director, Frank Lloyd), a tyrannical Captain Bligh has his ship taken away by the much-abused crew, led by its first mate, Fletcher Christian. The legacy of Richard King is a magnificent part of the American West.

In 1852, King, with profits from a riverboat company he helped create, started a cattle ranch in an area of Texas called Santa Gertrudis, near Corpus Christi. For $300, he received over 15,000 acres of land, and by 1861 he had 20,000 head of cattle. King bred a quality line of cattle — the Santa Gertrudis — which were a combination of Texas Longhorn and Eastern Durham. During the Civil War, he made a fortune supplying the Confederacy with armaments and livestock, among other things, through his riverboat operation. After the war, the King Ranch had expanded its cattle to 84,000 head; although it lost about 50,000 over several years to rustlers, by 1875 some 60,000 cattle were being driven annually to Kansas for shipment to market from a 600,000 acre empire.

Ten years earlier, a trader named Jesse Chisholm blazed a wagon trail from Kansas to Texas and brought word to many that cattle were wanted in the North. The great herds driven by a number of ranchers began moving into Abilene, Kansas, where one Joseph McCoy set up stockyards. The Union Pacific Railway, having reached Abilene in 1867, shipped the cattle to markets as far east as Chicago. In that first year, 35,000 head of cattle came into Abilene; four years later, 700,000 were brought to the cow town.

Near the Mexican border, in Elgin, Arizona, Hawks filmed the scenes of Dunson's vast cattle ranch. Much of the picture was shot in Rain Valley, Arizona, 60 miles from Tucson, including the sequence where the cattle are brought across the river. The San Pedro River substituted for the Red River, and five dams were built to bring the water level up for the crossing. According to Hawks, 1500 cattle were transported around for filming; some accounts attributed that as many as 6000 to 9000 head of cattle were rented at ten dollars a head.

The film's budget, between $1,750,000 and $2,000,000, went $800,000 over, and Hawks put the blame on having to take the cattle, cast and crew to each location. The financial problems put Monterey Productions out of action. Although completed in 1946, *Red River* was not released until July 1948. There were two reasons for the holdup — Hawks was withholding the picture from distribution, and filmmaker Howard Hughes claimed that the ending was a steal from his picture *The Outlaw*.

United Artists was set to distribute *Red River*, but Hawks felt he was being cheated and tried to cut a better deal with another studio. However, United Artists did not let this happen. As for *The Outlaw*, there is a scene where Doc Holliday shoots at Billy the Kid's ears, taunting him to draw. Hawks, who had worked on this material when he was involved with the production, used a similar scene for the ending to *Red River* when Dunson shoots at Matt, nicking his cheek, to force his gun hand. Fortunately, both John Wayne and editor Christian Nyby came to Hawks' assistance and worked the problem out with Hughes.

Despite the high cost of the picture, *Red River* earned $4,506,825 domestically, which made it one of the top-grossing films of the year. The film also earned two Academy Award nominations — for Writing (Motion Picture Story, Borden Chase), and Film Editing (Christian Nyby). Richard Schweizer and David Wechsler won the writing award for *The Search*, while Paul Weatherwax took the editing honor for Universal-International's *The Naked City*. The Directors Guild of America voted their second of four quarterly awards for the season to Howard Hawks for his majestic direction on *Red River*.

Hawks' specialty, on display in many of his films, is his depiction of group interaction; in this Western, it is the reason the cowboys succeed on the cattle drive. Only when Tom is willing to compromise does he become part of this group again. The final great images in *Red River* are of Matt walking to face Tom with the cowboys following, and of Dunson walking through the cattle to Matt.

John Wayne proved just what a remarkable actor he was in this first film for Hawks, a director whom he admired second only to John Ford. Duke's formidable Dunson was the first of many leathery and tough Western figures that he would play. *Look* magazine gave an achievement award to Montgomery Clift as "the most promising star on the Hollywood horizon" for his performances in *Red River* and *The Search*. The Western was also the senior Harry Carey's last, as he died in '47 before it was released.

Special mention must be made of Arthur Rosson, for sharing a co-director's credit; to Dimitri Tiomkin, for his stirring and lyrical score; and to Russell Harlan, for his breathtaking black-and-white photography. Although some feel the film is compromised by its ending, there is truly an authentic picture of cowboy life — of the dust, sweat and hardships on the trail. The bond between Tom Dunson and Matt Garth is inspiring. They might only be fictional characters, but certainly men like them existed. Bold, compassionate and even ruthless, they dared to risk everything for their vision of the American Dream.

Reviews

Variety: "Howard Hawks' production and direction have given a masterful interpretation to a story of the early West and the opening of the Chisholm Trail…"

New Yorker: "John Wayne, Montgomery Clift, Walter Brennan and John Ireland accompany the steers. Their performances are all first-rate."

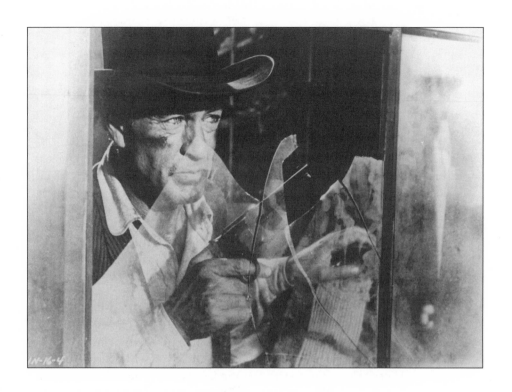

I'm not trying to be a hero. If you think I like this, you're crazy.

GARY COOPER *as Will Kane, to his wife Amy*

High Noon

1952

Gary Cooper as Will Kane.

HIGH NOON

A Stanley Kramer Production. Released by United Artists, 1952. Republic Pictures Home Video. 85 minutes.

Credits: Fred Zinnemann (Director); Stanley Kramer (Producer); Emmett Emerson (Assistant Director); Carl Foreman (Screenplay); Floyd Crosby (Photographer); Elmo Williams (Editor); Harry Gerstad (Editorial Supervisor); Rudolph Sternad (Production Designer); Ben Hayne (Art Director); Murray Waite (Set Decorator); Joe King (Men's Wardrobe); Ann Peck (Women's Wardrobe); Gustaf Norin (Makeup); Dimitri Tiomkin (Music Score). Song: "Do Not Forsake Me, Oh My Darlin'" by Dimitri Tiomkin, with lyrics by Ned Washington; sung by Tex Ritter. Based on the story *The Tin Star* by John W. Cunningham.

Cast: Gary Cooper (Will Kane); Thomas Mitchell (Jonas Henderson); Lloyd Bridges (Harvey Pell); Katy Jurado (Helen Ramirez); Grace Kelly (Amy Kane); Otto Kruger (Percy Mettrick); Lon Chaney, Jr. (Martin Howe); Henry Morgan (Sam Fuller); Ian MacDonald (Frank Miller); Eve McVeagh (Mildred Fuller); Harry Shannon (Cooper); Lee Van Cleef (Jack Colby); Robert Wilke (James Pierce); Sheb Wooley (Ben Miller); Tom London (Sam); Ted Stanhope (Station Master); Larry Blake (Gillis); William Phillips (Barber); Jeanne Blackford (Mrs. Henderson); James Millican (Baker); Cliff Clark (Weaver); Ralph Reed (Johnny); William Newell (Drunk); Lucien Prival (Bartender); Guy Beach (Fred); Howland Chamberlin (Hotel Clerk); Morgan Farley (Minister); Virginia Christine (Mrs. Simpson); Virginia Farmer (Mrs. Fletcher); Jack Elam (Charlie); Paul Dubov (Scott); Harry Harvey (Coy); Tim Graham (Sawyer); Nolan Leary (Lewis); Tom Greenway (Ezra); Dick Elliott (Kibbee); John Doucette (Trumbull).

Synopsis

One Sunday at 10:30 A.M., three gunmen on horseback ride into the Western town of Hadleyville. They are Jack Colby, Ben Miller and James Pierce. At the depot, the trio settles down to wait for the noon train.

In a nearby building, retiring marshal Will Kane is marrying his Quaker sweetheart, Amy. Officiating at the ceremony is Judge Mettrick, and among the attending friends are Jonas Henderson, Martin Howe and the Fullers. Will and Amy's joy is cut short by a telegram that says an old enemy of the marshal's, Frank Miller, will be coming in on the noon train. The three gunmen already at the station are Miller's cronies.

To avoid a confrontation, Will and Amy are encouraged by their friends to leave town immediately. Harvey Pell, a deputy, sees the couple ride off in their buckboard. With Harvey is Helen Ramirez, his girlfriend and a businesswoman in town. But Will realizes the folly of running away, and returns to town with Amy. He explains to her that Miller, sent to prison five years before on a murder charge and now released, would only follow them to their new ranch. Amy threatens to leave on the noon train because, as a Quaker, she is against violence.

The judge packs up and leaves town on horseback, remembering Miller had vowed to kill him and Will Kane.

Harvey wanted to become the new marshal, but Will didn't have the authority to give his deputy the position. Thinking Will could have helped, but didn't because Helen was Will's old flame, Harvey quits as deputy.

Helen, who had also been involved with Frank Miller, decides to sell her business and leave town; she advises the marshal that he should go away as well. Her reason for leaving, she tells Harvey, is that the whole town will die if Will is killed.

The hotel clerk liked Miller because business was better when he was around, and many of the townsmen in the saloon were his friends. Will is mocked when he tries to round up deputies from among the bar patrons.

Will goes to see his friend Sam Fuller, who pretends he is not at home, then asks for help from the church congregation. The parishioners debate the issue, and Jonas convinces them that getting involved in gunplay will hurt their Northern business interests which might build in Hadleyville. Jonas feels Will should leave town. So does Will's mentor Martin, who is crippled with arthritis in his hands and would be of no help to him in a gunfight against the outlaws.

Amy visits Helen to learn the truth about her and Will; she is told that their relationship is a thing of the past and that she should stand by her husband. Amy reveals to Helen that she became a Quaker because of the shooting deaths of her father and brother.

When the worried Will contemplates riding off, Harvey encourages him to do so and forces him into a fistfight. Will is battered badly but beats Harvey.

Feeling alienated and helpless, Will cries for a moment, and even writes his will. Townsman Herb Baker, a drunk and a teenage boy offered their help, but Will realizes the latter two would only be killed. Herb backs out when Will informs him there is no more help.

Everyone in town sits and waits solemnly until the train's whistle blows at noon; Will stands alone in the street as Amy and Helen pass together in a wagon bound for the train. Helen sees Frank join the other three gunmen at the station.

The four killers walk together through the streets of Hadleyville to confront Will. The marshal hides as they pass, calls out and, when they open fire, he shoots down Ben Miller. These first sounds of gunplay bring Amy running back.

Will uses hit-and-run tactics against the killers; while held up in a barn, he kills Colby. Frank sets the barn afire and Will creates a horse stampede to escape. He is shot off his fleeting mount but, not sustaining any serious injury, finds refuge in an empty store. Amy shoots Pierce in the back to save her husband, but Miller takes her hostage. Will is about to throw down his gun to save her when she breaks away, allowing him to finish off Miller.

Will and Amy embrace as the townsfolk come out to gather around them. Throwing his badge into the dirt, Will then climbs into the buckboard with his wife and rides out of town.

The Western genre was near or at its greatest in the 1950s, when so many classic pictures, both small and large scale, were produced. John Ford entered the decade with a personal favorite, RKO's *Wagonmaster*, then followed it with Republic's *Rio Grande*. Howard Hawks made *The Big Sky* in 1952 for RKO. The "B" Westerns began their decline in these early years due in no small part to the birth of television; ironically, the most famous of the "B" cowboys — William Boyd, Gene Autry and Roy Rogers — became even more popular in the new medium. Later in the decade, Hollywood used many different forms of wide screen vision and color photography to compete with the growing television market, but in these first years, black-and-white Westerns were the norm.

In 1950 alone, along with Ford's two pictures, there were two remarkable Westerns from 20th Century–Fox, *The Gunfighter* (Henry King, director) and the beautiful Technicolor *Broken Arrow* (Delmer Daves, director). Universal had *Winchester '73* (Anthony Mann, director), the first in a series of gritty, often revenge-motivated Westerns Mann made with James Stewart. Both *Winchester '73* and *The Gunfighter* dealt with the adult, psychological and socially oriented themes revitalized by *Stagecoach* in '39 and nurtured through the '40s, particularly by *The Ox-Bow Incident* and *Red River*. These themes were fully developed in the 1950s with the greatest black-and-white Western of the decade, *High Noon*.

Hollywood filmmakers finally presented the American Indian in a sympathetic light, most notably with *Broken Arrow*; in the '50s, Apaches and other tribesmen were given more dignity and not simply degraded as savages. Yet,

Gunmen walk the streets of Hadleyville in search of Kane. *Left to right:* **Sheb Woo-ley, Ian MacDonald, Lee Van Cleef, Robert Wilke.**

filmmakers were at the same time being shown a *lack* of understanding by the House Un-American Activities Committee for daring to be different. Carl Foreman, who wrote the screenplay for *High Noon*, was one of the victims; his script became an allegory of one man standing alone, living by his values and facing his fears. Producer Stanley Kramer and director Fred Zinnemann brought this allegory to life in the film, emphasizing the honor of the lone marshal standing up to a gang of men whose only aim is to bring him down. The great virtues of this film are its tremendous suspense, its famous ballad, and an excellent, understated performance from Gary Cooper which make it unforgettably haunting.

Gregory Peck had the title role in *The Gunfighter*; his also excellent and understated characterization of Jimmy Ringo was similar to the weary lawman in *High Noon*. Both men are sad victims of social ignorance and bear their heavy loads with as much dignity as they can muster. Although not given the same esteem as *High Noon, The Gunfighter* is every bit as good a Western. In fact, Peck turned down the role of Will Kane because he felt it was too similar to *The Gunfighter*.

Fred Zinnemann came to Hollywood in 1929, hoping to become a director.

He first worked as an extra in the great anti-war film *All Quiet on the Western Front* (released by Universal in '30; Lewis Milestone, director). By 1937, he was directing short subjects for MGM, and won an Oscar for the one-reeler *That Mothers Might Live*, which dealt with the work in obstetrics by Dr. Ignaz Philipp Semmelweiss. Zinnemann was given a seven-year MGM contract to direct feature length films — the first was the modest drama, *Kid Glove Killer* (1941). He won acclaim for two World War II-related dramas, 1944's *The Seventh Cross*, and 1948's *The Search*, for which he received an Academy Award nomination. When his contract expired, Zinnemann directed two films for independent producer Stanley Kramer, for release by United Artists — *The Men* (1950) and, of course, *High Noon*.

Kramer had organized his own production company, initially called Screen Plays, Inc., in 1947, with publicist George Glass and writer Carl Foreman. The company became Stanley Kramer Productions, Inc., after the success of two 1949 dramas with United Artists, *Champion* and *Home of the Brave*, directed by Mark Robson.

Zinnemann, Robson and Kramer were among the filmmakers whose daring films reflected sensitive social problems of this period. *Home of the Brave* dealt with a black soldier coping with racial discrimination during the Second World War, while *The Men* revealed the aftermath of war as an ex-soldier struggles with a physical disability from an injury sustained in the conflict. *High Noon*, although set in the Old West of the 1880s, was a reflection of the times in which it was filmed because of the investigations of the House Un-American Activities Committee (HUAC).

The Congress of the United States began the HUAC in 1938, prompted by the fear of Communism in America. By '47, HUAC chairman J. Parnell Thomas announced investigations into many different factions, including government and the film industry, to find Communists. Many filmmakers were accused of being subversives; a group known as the "Hollywood ten" was given jail sentences of six months to one year for their refusal to testify before the committee. "Blacklisting" began when others involved in the motion picture industry refused to employ the ten men. In 1951, Carl Foreman was called before the HUAC — at the time he had not only written the script for *High Noon*, but was its associate producer. Foreman denied being a Communist, but refused to say whether he had ever been one. This was in September — the same month filming on the Western had begun. After the shooting was completed in October, Foreman, for the sake of the picture, was no longer involved with Stanley Kramer Productions nor was he credited as associate producer. Literally, hundreds of Hollywood people were blacklisted for years, including Foreman. Much of the Communist "witch hunting" during the early 1950s was refueled by Senator Joseph McCarthy, who headed the Senate

Permanent Sub-Committee on Investigations. Although he was not part of HUAC, and instead focused on Communism in government, McCarthy's powerful influence was felt in Hollywood as well.

Carl Foreman's screenplay was based on the 1947 short story *The Tin Star* by John W. Cunningham. In this tale, Sheriff Doane is an old man with arthritic hands and Toby is his young deputy. They are waiting in town for the 4:10 P.M. train and a killer named Jordan, who has vowed to kill the sheriff for sending him to prison. Already in town and waiting to help Jordan are Frank Colby, young Jordan and Pierce. When Doane visits his deceased wife at the cemetery, young Jordan follows and scatters the sheriff's horse with gunshots. A chain of gunfire is then set off as Toby shoots down young Jordan, thinking Doane has been hit. Doane comes back and kills both Pierce and Colby. The sheriff and deputy have been wounded, however. Jordan, who has come in on the train, prepares to kill Toby, but Doane shields his deputy and takes the bullet instead. Toby finishes off Jordan before the sheriff succumbs to his wounds.

As early as 1948, Foreman had written an outline from the short story, with the marshal named Will Tyler and the returning ex-convict called Clyde Doyle. In a later outline, the screenwriter reverted to Cunningham's original names, Doane and Jordan. Finally, Doane became Will Kane and Jordan became Frank Miller. Of the other three badmen, Colby's first name was changed to Jack and young Jordan became Ben Miller (Frank's brother); only Pierce's name was left unchanged. Foreman believed nothing was to be gained by letting the hero die as he did in the original story; Doane's rhetoric here as he lies dying, that all a lawman has to show for his years is a tin star, is given in the film to the older retired marshal, Martin (and the crippling arthritis as well). Of course, the late wife of the sheriff became the very much alive Amy. While there is no Toby in the film to help the marshal, there is the embittered deputy Harvey, who takes a stand against the lawman.

A reference is made to another deputy not in town in the finished film. A sequence was actually shot in which this second deputy, played by James Brown, has a prisoner in tow outside town; the scene was not used because it apparently took away from the suspense and tension in Hadleyville. A sequence where Kane thinks of suicide as a way out of his ordeal was also dropped. This was thought to be the coward's way; instead, Kane was simply left to cry to show his fear and weariness.

The idea of having the film's actual running time correspond with the marshal's plight was Foreman's. The consensus by all was to keep the story as taut as possible. After the initial previews, Stanley Kramer had a series of shots made to show different clocks around town approaching noon, so as to further the tension. The use of the ballad "Do Not Forsake Me, Oh My Darlin'" was felt to be too repetitious, so it was tightened up for dramatic effect. Also added were close-ups of Gary Cooper's drawn face; in reality the actor was suffering from an ulcer (among other problems), which made the pain he felt as Will Kane all the more visible.

By 1952, Cooper had been a major Hollywood star for over 20 years, although his star quality in the years before *High Noon* had diminished slightly. He won an Academy Award as Best Actor (his second) for his performance. Playing a man of conscience caught between his sense of duty, his feelings of alienation from the people around him and his fear of almost certain death, Coop vividly displays humility and hurt. The role is justifiably his most famous.

Gary Cooper started out as an extra in silent pictures in 1925; his early appearances included a series of Paramount Westerns adapted from Zane Grey stories. By 1927, Coop had a contract with Paramount; his first starring Western was *Arizona Bound* (John Waters, director). That same year, he had a small role in *Wings* (William A. Wellman, director), the first motion picture to win the Academy Award for Best Picture. His first all-talking film was the 1929 Paramount Western, *The Virginian* (director, Victor Fleming). Already Coop was establishing the strong, soft-spoken Western figure with a boyish gleam that would help him become one of the most beloved of stars. For Paramount he was Wild Bill Hickok in Cecil B. DeMille's Western epic *The Plainsman* (1936); by 1940 he was with United Artists in *The Westerner* (director, William Wyler). Coop earned his first Oscar as Best Actor for *Sergeant York* the following year. While his heroic persona was richly appreciated in the early '40s, the rest of the decade and the first couple years of the 1950s found his career waning due to personal problems and several unrewarding films. Yet, in 1951, he had the good sense to follow the pioneering efforts made by his colleague James Stewart for *Winchester '73* a year earlier: He accepted a smaller salary plus a percentage of the gross for *High Noon*.

There are few if any classic Westerns that have not benefited from an exceptional supporting cast. The always commendable Thomas Mitchell, as Jonas, one of the town's leading citizens, never denies his admiration for Will, but lets it be known that the community's business interests come first. As Will's immature, self-serving deputy, Lloyd Bridges had one of his best roles; so too did Katy Jurado as Helen, who still has bittersweet feelings for the marshal, and confesses that she would not abandon him if she was his wife. Grace Kelly, as Amy, is forced to choose between her own religious convictions and her love for her husband. While the actress, at 22, was undeniably too young for Gary Cooper, who was then 50, their scenes together are filled with both spoken and unspoken emotions; aside from their embrace at the end, the only other happy moment they share is the wedding in the beginning which has a boyish Coop playfully teasing her. This fleeting joviality shows just how a young woman could fall in love with an older man. Kelly was supposedly disappointed with her performance, but it is a tender and touching one. Yet the film's most touching supporting performance, is given by Lon Chaney, Jr., who, as Kane's mentor and close friend, reflects sadly on a lawman's lot in life. The four badmen were played with cool menace by Ian MacDonald, Robert Wilke, Sheb Wooley and Lee Van Cleef.

The first image seen in *High Noon* is of Van Cleef, as Tex Ritter sings the theme song over the credits. This opening scene as Van Cleef waits for Wooley and Wilke to ride up was shot near Chatsworth, California, on the Iverson Ranch. In fact, the entire picture, although set in New Mexico, was filmed in California. The railway station where the three badmen wait for the noon train was shot on the renowned Sierra Railroad line at Warnerville. The Columbia Ranch in Burbank was used for the town of Hadleyville.

There were real lawmen like Will Kane in the Old West — they were needed after the Civil War in the new frontier cow towns like *Red River*'s Abilene, Kansas. When Tom Dunson rode into town in that film looking for a fight, there was no law as yet — only vigilantes existed. But in 1869, business leader Joseph McCoy helped in the election of a town council. A marshal, Tom "Bear River" Smith, was hired in '70 to enforce the council's laws, including barring guns in town. He didn't last six months, however, as he was killed making an arrest. Abilene was considered the wildest of cow towns when Smith was replaced by James Butler "Wild Bill" Hickok in 1871. Both were judged tough lawmen, but Smith was more temperate, preferring to use his fists instead of his guns to settle a dispute. Not so with Hickok, famed for his marksmanship; after killing two men needlessly, he was let go by the town council after only eight months service.

High Noon's marshal, Kane was also chosen by a council of community leaders. Apparently they could fire him at will, and he had the authority to make the citizenry help him in any emergency. Hence, the story probably could not have happened the way it did in *High Noon* if there had been a more assertive marshal or council.

Before Carl Foreman and Stanley Kramer ended their association, another partner, Sam Katz, a former executive with MGM, had been brought into the fold. It was expected that Stanley Kramer Productions would continue with stronger input at United Artists; however, the independent company joined Columbia in 1951 while producing *High Noon* for UA to culminate a five-picture deal. The Western was also backed by a business associate, Bruce Church, who had helped to finance some of Kramer's earlier films. The film, budgeted at $750,000, grossed $3,400,000 domestically, making it one of 1952's hits following a July release.

High Noon was nominated for seven Academy Awards: Best Picture, Actor,

Director, Screenplay, Film Editing, Song and Scoring of a Dramatic or Comedy Picture. There were four winners. Cooper won, of course, and Elmo Williams and Harry Gerstad won for their editing efforts. The other two wins were for the song "Do Not Forsake Me, Oh My Darlin'" (music by Dimitri Tiomkin, lyrics by Ned Washington) and for the score. *The Greatest Show on Earth*, the Cecil B. DeMille circus epic, won for Best Picture; Charles Schnee's script for *The Bad and the Beautiful* (Vincente Minnelli, director) won over Foreman's screenplay; and John Ford bested Fred Zinnemann as director for his work on Republic's *The Quiet Man*. Zinnemann did win the New York Film Critics Award as Best Director, as did the film for Best Picture.

Zinnemann's artistic sensitivity greatly enhanced *High Noon*, although there were friends who felt, prior to production, that a Western would not be his forte. But he definitely believed in the simple story of one man's courage, and he made good use of Gary Cooper's image to represent the ideal of the individual faithfully adhering to conscience. The noble theme of a man maintaining his dignity in the face of adversity was Zinnemann's forte. Director and actor created a bond in following Will Kane's struggle, as did Carl Foreman, who certainly went through a great deal of personal struggle of his own. The ultimate satisfaction comes from knowing their respective stories have withstood the test of time. A CBS-TV movie sequel *High Noon, Part II: The Return of Will Kane* (director, Jerry Jameson; and starring Lee Majors) was made in 1980. It attempted (with only average results) to recreate the fine acting and suspense of the original film.

The captivating suspense and swift action were an extremely large part of the success of the '52 Western. Williams and Gerstad's editing contributed mightily to the unrelenting pace. Floyd Crosby, with his stark photography of a desolate Western community with a ghost town eeriness, gave the film an almost documentary feel.

Tex Ritter's gentle, melancholic singing of the ballad off and on throughout the picture seemed like a specter accompanying Cooper's lone figure. One of the film's most famous scenes is the "crane" shot with the camera slowly pulling back and up to show Coop standing all by himself in the deserted street. The memory of everything about *High Noon* is haunting because it gives, with its sparse look, a sense of being frightfully alone and facing the terrible ordeal with Will Kane on a dusty little street somewhere long ago.

Reviews

Commonweal: "*High Noon* wins a place next to *Stagecoach* as a first-rate Western; and for its intelligent themes, social significance and high entertainment values, it is outstanding in any category."

The New York Times: "In a style of consummate realism, Mr. Zinnemann has done a splendid job.... And so has the cast, under his direction. Mr. Cooper is at the top of his form in a type of role that has trickled like water off his back for years."

You go home to your mother and your father, and grow up to be strong and straight. And, Joey, take care of them — both of them

ALAN LADD *as Shane*

Shane

1953

Alan Ladd (left) and Brandon de Wilde.

SHANE

A George Stevens Production. A Paramount Picture, 1953.
Technicolor. Paramount Home Video. 117 minutes.

Credits: George Stevens (Director and Producer); Ivan Moffat (Associate Producer); A.B. Guthrie, Jr. (Screenplay); Jack Sher (Additional Dialogue); Loyal Griggs (Photographer); Irmin Roberts (Second Unit Photographer); William Hornbeck, Tom McAdoo (Editors); Hal Pereira, Walter Tyler (Art Directors); Emile Kuri (Set Decorator); Edith Head (Costumes); Gordon Jennings (Special Effects); Victor Young (Music Score). Based on the novel by Jack Schaefer.

Cast: Alan Ladd (Shane); Jean Arthur (Marion Starrett); Van Heflin (Joe Starrett); Brandon de Wilde (Joey); Walter Jack Palance (Wilson); Ben Johnson (Chris); Edgar Buchanan (Lewis); Emile Meyer (Ryker); Elisha Cook, Jr. (Torrey); Douglas Spencer (Shipstead); John Dierkes (Morgan); Ellen Corby (Mrs. Torrey); Paul McVey (Grafton); John Miller (Atkey); Edith Evanson (Mrs. Shipstead); Leonard Strong (Wright); Ray Spiker (Johnson); Janice Carroll (Susan Lewis); Martin Mason (Howell); Helen Brown (Mrs. Lewis); Nancy Kulp (Mrs. Howell); Howard J. Negley (Pete); Beverly Washburn (Ruth Lewis); Charles Quirk (Clerk); George J. Lewis, Jack Sterling, Henry Wills, Rex Moore, Ewing Brown, Chester W. Hannan, Bill Cartledge, Steve Raines (Ryker Men).

Synopsis

A man on horseback rides onto a small homestead, watched by a playful boy. The child, Joey, lives there with his folks, Joe and Marion Starrett. The homesteader mistakes the stranger for one of a group of cowboys, led by a cattleman named Ryker, who have come to tell the Starretts to get off the land as it's needed for open range. When the stranger sides with Joe, saying he is a friend, the Ryker bunch heeds the farmer's demands to get off his homestead. Calling himself Shane, the stranger is invited to supper by the Starretts. Shane's swift and sudden moves to his holstered gun make it obvious to the family that he is a gunfighter.

Knowing that Joe is trying to uproot a massive and stubborn tree stump on the farm, Shane begins chopping away at it with an ax after supper. Soon he and the farmer work at it together until it is unearthed. The two men have bonded. Joey particularly takes a liking to Shane.

The following morning, Shane accepts Joe's offer to stay on as a hired hand, much to Joey's satisfaction. Shane takes the buckboard into town to pick up some wire for Joe and some work clothes for himself. Another farmer, Ernie Wright, visits Joe, informing him that he intends to pull out with his family because Ryker's men have damaged his crop.

Meanwhile, in town, Shane runs into one of Ryker's men, Chris. Taking Joe's advice to steer clear of any trouble, Shane allows the man to humiliate him.

At a meeting, Shane is introduced to the other farmers; among them are Lewis and Torrey, who now believe he is a coward. Joe defends him, however, and calls for unity against Ryker.

When the homesteaders travel together into town to pick up supplies, Shane is bothered again by Chris. A fistfight ensues with Shane beating the cowboy. Ryker offers Shane a job, which he refuses. The cattleman and his men begin beating on him, but Joe comes to Shane's aid and together they defeat Ryker's men in a donnybrook. Immediately afterwards, Ryker sends for a gunfighter.

The Starretts have become very attached to Shane. Marion feels an unspoken affection for him, and Joey admits to loving him.

A gunfighter, Wilson, arrives in town on Independence Day. Ernie has decided to leave because the cowboys continue to destroy his homestead. Shane begins to teach Joey how to shoot, but Marion is against it, feeling the valley would be better off without guns.

When Joe and Marion return to their homestead after a holiday festivity, Ryker is waiting there with Wilson and offers Joe a job. Ryker and Joe argue over the rights to the land, and the farmer points out that the government backs the homesteaders.

When Torrey returns to town on another day, he is enticed to draw his gun against Wilson, who then kills him. Ryker believes this action will scare the farmers away.

Lewis' home is burned by the cowboys while he is attending Torrey's funeral. The other homesteaders agree to rebuild it. Both Shane and Joe speak at the funeral that the farmers have a right to raise their families in the valley.

Joe realizes that Ryker has to be stopped; when the cattleman's brother Morgan comes to the Starrett home to set up a meeting, the farmer agrees to come later that night to town. But Chris tells Shane that it is a trap.

Shane wishes to go instead because gunfighting is something he understands, and he has to fight Joe to do it. To stop his friend, Shane is forced to knock him unconscious with his gun. Joey tells Shane he hates him for hitting his father. Marion asks Shane if he is doing this just for her and he replies that it is for Joe and Joey as well. She bids him farewell.

Shane (Alan Ladd) teaches Joey (Brandon de Wilde) to shoot.

Joey follows Shane into town and sees him standing against Wilson and Ryker. Shane outdraws both his enemies, and only Joey's warning saves him from more than a slight wound from a backshooting Morgan. Having killed all three men, Shane looks sadly at the carnage and walks away to his horse. Joey is waiting and tells Shane he is sorry for saying he hated him.

When the boy asks him to return home, Shane explains how he cannot, that there is no going back from a killing, that he must be honest to his mold as a gunfighter. As he rides away, Joey cries out to him to come back. But Shane rides out of the valley.

By the early 1950s, motion pictures were competing with the new television markets. Western films were not excluded. The DuMont network had broadcasted the *Western Movie* as early as 1946; *The Lone Ranger* and *Hopalong Cassidy* began airing in 1949. Gene Autry came to television in 1950 on CBS, and Roy Rogers followed a year later on NBC. These programs were, of course, geared for the young and the young-at-heart with their bigger-than-life heroes. "B" Western films declined in the '50s because television had taken over their territory. Although the "B" format tried to stay tall in the saddle — there were a series of singing Rex Allen Westerns for Republic, and a number of Bill Elliott vehicles for Monogram, among others — television was just too attractive a lure for audiences. Both the Allen and Elliott films were prime examples of the way the genre had evolved — Allen in the lighter vein of an Autry or Rogers, and Elliott in a hard-hitting niche of a Wayne or Cooper.

Perhaps then it was no mere coincidence that *Shane* came in 1953. Here was a hero of the ages, personifying all that was noble and pure, yet blemished by his reputation as a deadly gunfighter. The "A" Western may have reached its ultimate aim with this film.

The wide screen effect in films became a necessity in the fight against the TV medium; *Shane* features glorious panoramic vistas of mountains, sky and surrounding countryside. Producer-director George Stevens created an epic of heartfelt beauty and mythologized the American West as no other film, and this despite its timeworn theme of cattlemen against homesteaders. But what really makes the film so special is the way it develops through the eyes of an impressionable little boy, who experiences with hero worship the legend of Shane. The acting by everyone in this movie is simply marvelous.

Shane came the year after *High Noon*, and these two are the most famous of all Westerns. Another film in '53, *Hondo* (Warner Bros.; John Farrow, director), bears a resemblance to *Shane*. Filmed in the 3-D process, *Hondo* starred John Wayne as a rougher version of Alan Ladd's Shane, although both heroes not only wear a buckskin shirt and a white hat, but share an indomitable spirit to help a struggling frontier family. While *Hondo* did not rival *Shane* in popularity nor acclaim, it was an outstanding Western of the early 1950s.

The meticulous craftsmanship of filmmaker Stevens was his trademark. Coming to Hollywood in 1929, Stevens directed a series of Hal Roach comedy shorts before moving on to feature length films in the '30s. In 1935 he directed his only Western prior to *Shane*, RKO's lively *Annie Oakley*; Stevens' most famous film of this early period was the 1939 action adventure *Gunga Din*. During the 1940s, he made a series of comedies, two of them — *The Talk of the Town* ('42) and *The More the Merrier* ('43) — co-starring his *Shane* leading lady, Jean Arthur. He won an Oscar as Best Director in 1951 for Paramount's drama *A Place in the Sun*, starring Montgomery Clift.

Stevens began filming *Shane* in the summer of '51 in Jackson Hole, Wyoming, and principal photography was completed in the fall. Yet another 16 months of painstaking post-production followed at Paramount before the film was ready for its April '53 release.

His romanticized look at the spirit of the Old West was both tender and enthralling, and its violence brutally realistic — as was Jack Schaefer's 1949 novel on which it was based. *Shane* (the book and film) is basically a tale of good versus evil. In the novel, Shane had dark hair and wore dark clothes; Stevens chose to make his gunfighter more dashing in bright buckskin and blond hair. In both versions, Shane is soft-spoken and rather slight of build. The character telling the tale in the novel was the homesteaders' boy, now named Bob and grown, looking back in time. The cattle baron in the novel is called Fletcher, and Morgan is his foreman, not his brother.

Shane's fistfight with Chris in the book is more vicious (he breaks the cowboy's arm), as is the brawl the other cowboys have with Joe Starrett and Shane (who is badly hurt and carried away in the farmer's arms). But the savage killing of a farmer by the hired killer, Wilson, is more powerful in the film, as the gunman's crushing bullets send the victim's body hurtling backwards. This scene was accomplished by attaching a wire to Elisha Cook's body and yanking it at the right moment (the same procedure was used on Jack Palance's Wilson when he is shot by Shane). In the book, Ernie Wright, not Torrey, is Wilson's victim. There is no slugfest between Joe and Shane in the novel, but the farmer is knocked cold with a gun to prevent him from facing Wilson. In the novel, Wilson and Fletcher are killed by Shane, but not Morgan. Bob watches Shane ride away at the book's end, yet, unlike Joey, does not call out for him to come back. After Shane has gone in the novel, Chris asks Joe for his job as hired hand.

A romantic attraction between Shane and Marion Starrett is touched upon in both novel and film, but only lightly. Alan Ladd and Jean Arthur are very low-keyed and even gentle in these roles; she is mostly tender and gracious throughout. Ladd is called upon to reveal a blunt, violent nature to Shane when there is need of it. Ladd with his trademark stoicism and handsome features perfectly embodies the spirit of Shane.

Coming to Hollywood in the 1930s, Alan Ladd found work as a bit player and grip. His first appearance in a Western was in a 1937 John Wayne "B", *Born to the West* (Paramount; Charles Barton, director). With the help of his agent Sue Carol (later his wife), Ladd would win a Paramount contract; he became a star playing a cool killer in 1942's gangster drama, *This Gun for Hire* (Frank Tuttle, director). He had his first Western lead for Paramount in 49's *Whispering Smith* (director, Leslie Fenton). He made two more for the studio in the early '50s, *Branded* (Rudolph Mate, director) and *Red Mountain* (William Dieterle, director). Although the Western *The Iron Mistress* (Gordon Douglas, director; with Ladd as the legendary Jim Bowie) was made after *Shane*, it was released in 1952 under a new contract with Warner Bros.

Jean Arthur started her acting career in silent films during the '20s; in 1936, she was Calamity Jane with Gary Cooper in *The Plainsman*. She bustled with energy in her films. In 1936's slice of modern Americana *Mr. Deeds Goes to Town*, she was with Coop again; she co-starred with James Stewart in its 1939 companion piece, *Mr. Smith Goes to Washington*. (Both of these dramas were directed by Frank Capra for Columbia.) In '41, she was in the Columbia Western, *Arizona* (director, Wesley Ruggles). In 1943, ten years before the release of *Shane*, Arthur earned an Oscar nomination as Best Actress in Stevens' *The More the Merrier*.

Van Heflin won the Oscar for Best Supporting Actor in MGM's 1942 drama *Johnny Eager* (Mervyn LeRoy, director). The versatility of this superb character actor was demonstrated when he played the stubborn and proud Joe Starrett in *Shane*. His scenes with Alan Ladd as they stand gallantly together to uproot that old stump, and later battle the cowboys, display a genuine camaraderie; the two actors became lifelong friends.

But *Shane*'s finest performance came from young Brandon de Wilde, whose all-American looks, exuberance and spirit of innocence made him an ideal choice for Joey. His every expression is filled with curiosity and wonder; de Wilde received an Academy Award nomination as Best Supporting Actor.

Ladd's evil counterpart as a gunfighter, Wilson, was a part Jack Palance thoroughly relished — his dark, lean and smoldering presence here radiates menace. He was also given an Oscar nomination as Best Supporting Actor. As Chris, the cowpoke whose bluster earns him a painful yet rewarding lesson in manhood from Shane, Ben Johnson had one of his finest roles.

The feisty screen personality of Elisha Cook, Jr., was never better, as his hot temper as Torrey brings him to a tragic end. His murder in the film is the catalyst which prompts the final gunplay. One of *Shane*'s most moving sequences is this farmer's burial, as the other homesteaders come together in an overwhelming feeling of unity.

The man trying to force the families from their homes is cattle baron Ryker, who has the same single-minded selfishness that befell Tom Dunson in *Red River*. The solid playing by Emile Meyer brings out this ruthlessness, but there is a trace of sympathy for him because, again like Dunson, he represents the rancher who feels he has won the land through long years of hardship, including bloodshed.

In 1862, President Abraham Lincoln signed the Homestead Act put forth by the U.S. Congress. This law gave settlers free ownership of Western farmland if they lived and worked on it for five years. Trouble developed between homesteaders and cattlemen in different areas, including Wyoming. As related in *Shane*, farmers had their own irrigation, taking the water supply away from the rancher's cattle, and they put up fences to keep the herds off their lands. In 1892, Wyoming ranchers hired a team of gunfighters to ride roughshod over the homesteaders; ironically, the farmers banded together and actually bested the ranchers and gunmen. In *Shane*, the effectiveness of the farmers' stand against Ryker is due to Joe's bullheadedness and Shane's gun.

The famous gunfighters of the Old West — like Billy the Kid and Tom Horn — have a romantic aura, much like Ladd's Shane, because of stories and films about them. But in reality, they were as ruthless as Palance's Wilson. Both Tom Horn and Billy the Kid were involved in range disputes. The Kid was a gunman in New Mexico and sided with a cattleman named John Tunstall, who was killed in a 1878 power struggle with a rival rancher, Lawrence Murphy. Wyoming cattle barons hired Horn as a "regulator" to hunt down rustlers; the gunfighter was hanged in 1903 for the killing of a sheepherder's boy. Some say he was framed.

Produced for $3,000,000, *Shane* made $9,000,000 in domestic earnings, making it the most successful Western of the 1950s. Besides the two Best Supporting Actor nods, the film received four other Oscar nominations — Best Picture, Director, Screenplay (A.B. Guthrie, Jr.), and Cinematography (Color; Loyal Griggs). Only Griggs was a winner for his beautiful photography; especially majestic are Wyoming's Grand Teton Mountains, with the mysterious aura complementing the mystique of Shane. Nineteen fifty-three was the year for Columbia's army drama *From Here to Eternity*— it won the Oscars for Best Picture, Director (Fred Zinnemann), Screenplay (Daniel Taradash), and Supporting Actor (Frank Sinatra). However, George Stevens was honored as a filmmaker by the Academy of Motion Picture Arts and Sciences with the Irving G. Thalberg Memorial Award.

The American West was never better represented in cinematic art than in *Shane*. Stevens' production is perfection; each camera composition is framed like a painting. (Some critics felt that Stevens' style was too mechanized.) Apart from the high quality of its direction, acting, photography, editing (William Hornbeck and Tom McAdoo) and lovely sentimental score (Victor Young), *Shane's* true greatness lies in the way it told its simple story with eloquence.

Joey's idolization of Shane is the key to the mystique here, as every viewer with memories of childhood innocence and heroes would attest. The boy is feeling what we must all feel in order for *Shane* to be called the best of its kind. Although Joey knows right from wrong, good from bad, it is not entirely wise for Joey to admire a gunfighter, even Shane, who sacrifices his dreams so that the homesteaders might achieve their own. Shane would very much like to remain one of them, but once he uses his gun to kill, he realizes he cannot.

The gun in this film is treated like a tool of conflicting forces. When Shane shows Joey how to shoot, the gun's power threatens to open the earth itself, which it very well does for the farmer murdered by Wilson (one of the most powerful screen deaths up to this time), and for Shane who has no recourse but to use it again to protect those he has come to love. It is a sad yet heartwarming thing to see Shane say farewell to Marion and then to Joey; many tears have been shed by the time Alan Ladd rides away, slumped over in the saddle, heartsick that he must leave their valley. Yet leave he must to be true to the Western myth. The complete sacrifice from Shane comes from knowing that to hold on to this myth, the decline of gunslingers in the Old West just had to be. If in spirit only, *Shane* indisputably holds the laurels for its thoughtfulness of an American heritage.

Reviews

Commonweal: "Producer-director George Stevens has taken this theme (which has been worn to triteness by many a mediocre movie) and restated it with freshness and a curious mixture of earthiness and mysticism. He is considerably aided by a good script (by A.B. Guthrie, Jr.) and by an outstanding cast for whose fine performances Stevens is no doubt responsible."

Newsweek: "If *Shane* is on the fabulous side, Ladd gives in his portrayal of him the best performance in his screen career. Time after time Stevens invests the screenplay with imaginative and realistic details that are little short of brilliant. And his use of Technicolor (with Loyal Griggs at the camera) is a masterpiece of illustration and mood-making."

*So we'll find them in the end, I promise you. We'll
find them, just as sure as the turning of the earth.*

JOHN WAYNE *as Ethan Edwards,
speaking to Martin about the Comanches*

The Searchers

1956

Left to right: Natalie Wood, John Wayne, and Jeffrey Hunter.

THE SEARCHERS

A C.V. Whitney Picture. A Warner Bros. Presentation, 1956. Technicolor. VistaVision. Warner Home Video. 119 minutes.

Credits: John Ford (Director); Merian C. Cooper (Executive Producer); Patrick Ford (Associate Producer); Wingate Smith (Assistant Director); Frank S. Nugent (Screenplay); Winton C. Hoch (Photographer); Alfred Gilks (Second Unit Photographer); Jack Murray (Editor); Frank Hotaling, James Basevi (Art Directors); Victor Gangelin (Set Decorator); Frank Beetson, Ann Peck (Costumes); George Brown (Special Effects); Max Steiner (Music Score). Title song by Stan Jones; sung by the Sons of the Pioneers. Based on the novel by Alan LeMay.

Cast: John Wayne (Ethan Edwards); Jeffrey Hunter (Martin Pawley); Vera Miles (Laurie Jorgensen); Ward Bond (Captain/Reverend Samuel Clayton); Natalie Wood (Debbie Edwards); John Qualen (Lars Jorgensen); Olive Carey (Mrs. Jorgensen); Henry Brandon (Chief Scar); Ken Curtis (Charlie McCorry); Harry Carey, Jr. (Brad Jorgensen); Antonio Moreno (Emilio Figueroa); Hank Worden (Mose Harper); Beulah Archuletta (Look); Walter Coy (Aaron Edwards); Dorothy Jordan (Martha Edwards); Pippa Scott (Lucy Edwards); Pat Wayne (Lt. Greenhill); Lana Wood (Debbie, as a Child); Jack Pennick (Private); Peter Mamakos (Futterman); Bill Steele (Nesby); Cliff Lyons (Col. Greenhill); Chuck Roberson (Man at Wedding); Ruth Clifford (Deranged Woman at Fort); Mae Marsh (Woman at Fort); Dan Borzage (Accordionist at Funeral). Also Billy Cartledge, Chuck Hayward, Slim Hightower, Fred Kennedy, Frank McGrath, Dale Van Sickel, Henry Wills, Terry Wilson, Away Luna, Billy Yellow, Bob Many Mules, Exactly Sonnie Betsuie, Feather Hat, Jr., Harry Black Horse, Jack Tin Horn, Many Mules Son, Percy Shooting Star, Pete Grey Eyes, Pipe Line Begishe, Smile White Sheep.

Synopsis

A cabin door opens upon a Texas horizon and a woman and her family step outside to view an approaching horseman. The rider is Ethan Edwards, returning home after several years to his brother Aaron's ranch. The woman is Aaron's wife Martha, and their children are Lucy, Ben and Debbie. Martin Pawley is also a member of the family, having been raised by Aaron and Martha after Ethan found him years before, the lone survivor of an Indian massacre.

Ethan is intolerant of Martin because of his Indian blood. A Confederate soldier in the Civil War, Ethan guards his past mysteriously as it is now 1868; he has waited three years after the war to return home and in his possession are freshly minted gold coins. Martha seems to have a need to also keep Ethan's past a secret.

The next morning, Captain Samuel Clayton arrives at the Edwards' home with a posse of Texas Rangers. Ethan and Martin join them in a search for cattle stolen from the nearby Jorgensen Ranch. Lucy and Lars Jorgensen's son Brad are in love. Before departing, Clayton, who is also the community's minister sees Martha lovingly embracing Ethan's coat before giving it to him.

Out in the desert, Ethan and the others find the cattle dead (one bull has a Comanche lance in it), and they realize it was a ruse to lure them away as the Indians are on a murder raid. Most of the posse then sets out for the nearby Jorgensen spread where Lars' wife and daughter Laurie are; Ethan and a crazed old man, Mose Harper, rest their horses before returning to Aaron's home 40 miles away. Martin races off, not heeding Ethan's warning to rest his mount. He is afoot as the other two men later ride past.

Ethan finds the ranch burning to the ground, Aaron, Martha and Ben murdered, and Lucy and Debbie kidnapped. A funeral is held, but Ethan ends it abruptly to go after the girls with the Rangers joining him.

In the night, they try to sneak up on the Comanches, but find their campsite abandoned. The Comanches later find them and surround the Rangers; there is a wild chase and a fight and the Indians are driven off. Ethan continues to shoot them as they carry off their dead, and he is stopped by Clayton. Having had enough of Clayton's interference, Ethan ventures on with only Martin and Brad. The remaining Rangers return home.

The trio continue their search and find that the Comanches have broken their trail, with four horses cutting off into a valley. Ethan follows and comes riding out the far side a bit bewildered. Brad and Martin are waiting for him, having circled around the valley, and they notice Ethan has lost his coat.

Finding the Indians' campsite later, Brad insists he has seen Lucy among them. But Ethan corrects him by saying it is a Comanche buck wearing her dress, that he found Lucy dead back in the valley and buried her in his coat. Brad goes berserk, rushes after the Comanches and is killed.

Ethan and Martin continue their search until they lose the Comanches' trail in the snow. They turn back temporarily to the Jorgensen spread. The Jorgensens show Ethan a letter containing a piece of material from an apron Debbie wore. Ethan rides out the following morning without Martin. Laurie, who is smitten with Martin, shows him the letter, which is from a trader named Futterman. Martin is fond of Laurie, too, but rides off after Ethan.

Martin catches up to Ethan and together they find Futterman. The trader,

Left to right: **Jeffrey Hunter, John Wayne, and Harey Carey, Jr., have formed a search party in the desert.**

who is only interested in the $1,000 reward offered for Debbie's return, informs the searchers that a war chief named Scar has taken her captive.

Later that night, while Martin and Ethan are camped, Futterman and two other men try to ambush them for the reward money. Ethan uses an unknowing Martin as bait to ensnare and kill the ambushers.

After much time passes, Ranger Charlie McCorry brings Laurie a letter from Martin. It relates how Martin, trading for a blanket at an Indian agency, mistakenly bought himself an Indian wife named Look. Martin, not wanting her around, treated her rudely. She did leave after Ethan and Martin questioned her about Chief Scar, but left a marker for them to follow.

When the two men came across a buffalo herd in the snow, Ethan savagely shot down as many of the animals as he could to keep the Comanches from having them for food and clothing. Martin was appalled at this and also by a cavalry attack on the Indians which left Look among the dead.

At the cavalry outpost, there was no sign of Scar or Debbie, but Ethan's hatred for the Indians was all the more apparent as he looked with disgust at the insane ramblings of another white captive. The searchers then followed Scar's trail into the New Mexico territory.

All this information is in Martin's letter to Laurie, who is so upset that she turns to Charlie for comfort. Martin and Ethan run into old Mose, and he introduces them to a Mexican named Emilio Figueroa who knows Scar. For a price, Emilio takes them to the Indian. In the guise of traders, the searchers meet Scar and see Debbie, now a teenager and one of the chief's wives. They learn from Scar that he took white lives for the murders of two sons by white men. Realizing that Scar knows who the searchers are, Emilio wants no part of the blood money from a vengeful Ethan.

Camped by a creek, Ethan and Martin are soon joined by Debbie. Although remembering her childhood, Debbie tells them that her place is now with the Indians. Ethan is set to shoot her, but Martin shields her body with his own. A Comanche arrow suddenly strikes Ethan in the shoulder, stopping him from hurting Debbie.

The two men are forced to flee without Debbie, and they hold off the attacking Comanches from a cave. Later, Martin helps Ethan with his wound.

On the night of Laurie's wedding to Charlie, Martin and Ethan return to the Jorgensen home. A fight over Laurie breaks out between Charlie and Martin. Laurie does truly love Martin, so Charlie calls a halt to the wedding. Moments later, cavalry/officer Lt. Greenhill arrives with urgent news for Captain Clayton: Mose has been rescued after being a prisoner of Scar. The old man alerts them that the Comanches have returned to the area.

Clayton and the other Texas Rangers ride out after the Indians, with Martin and Ethan acting as scouts. Laurie had earlier told Martin that Ethan's bullet was the best thing for Debbie since she now lived as a squaw.

Martin is determined to bring Debbie back; he convinces Clayton and Ethan to give him time to get her out before they come charging into Scar's camp. Debbie is willing to return with Martin, but he is forced to shoot down Scar. The gunfire acts as a signal for Ethan, the Rangers and Greenhill's cavalry to ride quickly into the midst of the Comanches. The Indians are soon defeated. Ethan, finding Scar's body, takes his scalp.

Ethan then chases after Debbie; upon catching her, he realizes that he cannot kill his niece because his love is stronger than any hate. While Clayton is being tended for a saber cut in his buttocks from Lt. Greenhill, Ethan carries Debbie in his arms back to the Jorgensens. She is welcomed into their home by them as Ethan stands on the porch. Martin also goes inside with Laurie. Ethan looks inside the home. Holding his arm, Ethan turns and walks away as the door slowly is closed.

By the middle of the 1950s, the adult Western was represented in both "A" and "B" films, and on television as well. In 1955, "A" Westerns included 20th Century–Fox's *The Tall Men* (Raoul Walsh, director) and the final Anthony Mann/James Stewart film, *The Man from Laramie* (Columbia). In the "B" format, Audie Murphy was the most popular Western star. And television in 1955 was on the trail of adult themes with the premieres of ABC's *The Life and Legend of Wyatt Earp* and CBS's *Gunsmoke*. Serious adult stories were also seen on television in the syndicated anthology series, *Death Valley Days*.

Many of these Westerns seemed to have one thing in common — a protagonist making a single-minded, often relentless stand against an injustice, or at the least a wrong that goes against that individual's own rigid code. With the more three-dimensional Western heroes in the '50s, it was natural for the greatest of all Western directors, John Ford, to epitomize this with the greatest of all Western stars, John Wayne. Their collaboration on 1956's *The Searchers* is regarded by many of their admirers to be their finest achievement.

Here is a hero, Ethan Edwards, with the mythic proportions of Shane in that he is a bigger-than-life creation. Unlike Shane, whose drawback was being a gunfighter, Ethan's failings are far more complex. A man who rides into a frontier community with a mysterious past like Shane, Ethan becomes obsessed with hatred because of the people around him. Shane's change was not one of hatred but of sadness that the reaction must be partially violent. The strongest feelings that connect the films are Ethan's and Shane's ultimate loneliness and the frontier isolation that engulfs all. The sweeping beauty of the land in each shows the irresistible pull that it has on the people. Also shown is the fury of the wilderness.

While more of the latter film's atmosphere comes from the haunting isolation, it is in turn reflected with more tragic consequences through the isolated, tortured soul of Ethan. John Ford called *The Searchers* "the tragedy of a loner," and so often the power of it comes from this character's unspoken yet painful expressions of love and hate.

Like the massive rock formations in Ford's cherished Monument Valley (never utilized to better effect), Ethan, too, seems like an extension of the very earth. He is symbolic of the fortitude and racism of this time and place in a West where survival sometimes meant fighting the land and hostile Indians. The juxtaposition of man's spirit with nature is what makes *The Searchers* the ultimate Ford-Wayne Western. Four years earlier, Ford won his fourth and last Academy Award as Best Director for the enchanting film, *The Quiet Man*. This beloved Irish tale with Duke Wayne (and Ward Bond) is considered to be their best non–Western together. Ford also won two additional Oscars for his World War II documentaries.

The Searchers was originally a 1954 novel by Alan LeMay. In the novel, Ethan is called Amos, and he is already involved with the hunt for the stolen cattle at the story's beginning. With him are Martin Pauley and other Texans, including Charlie MacCorry and Mose Harper; they are simply fellow neighbors, not Rangers, and there is no Sam Clayton. Amos' brother is named Henry, and he and wife Martha have a fourth child, an older son, Hunter. Lars Jorgensen is Aaron Mathison in the book, and he and his wife have two additional sons named Abner and Tobe. Even Mose has a son, Zack, but a character named Lije Powers leads the nomadic existence of the film's Mose Harper. In LeMay's story, Ethan was the name of Martin's late father, who was killed with Martin's mother and two sisters in an Indian massacre, while Martin was found as a baby by Henry Edwards. Martin is the book's main character.

As in the film, the actual attack on the Edwards' ranch is not revealed, only the harrowing aftermath — the two girls, Lucy and Debbie, are kidnapped, and the others are killed and scalped. During the community's initial search for the girls, Martin realizes Amos was in love with Martha; a neighbor, Ed Newby, is badly hurt in the first fight with the Comanches (and later commits suicide). In the movie, it is a character named Nesby who is wounded but he doesn't kill himself. Brad Mathison goes on with Martin and Amos and is killed, although Amos finds Lucy's body on a rock shelf. The only letter Martin writes in LeMay's story is one to the Mathisons regarding Brad's death.

Amos is given a letter by Aaron Mathison from a trader called Futterman; as in the film, the searchers first learn of Chief Scar through the trader, who is killed trying to ambush them. While Martin is not as rude to Look as is his screen counterpart, he does ignore her advances; after 11 days, she disappears with another Comanche.

The searchers come across the cavalry massacre of a band of Comanches just like in the movie. LeMay writes that an Osage Indian spoke to Martin and Amos about the tribe led by Bluebonnet (Scar is supposedly one of the war chiefs), but neither Indian nor Debbie are found with the cavalry.

At a barn party back home, Martin and Charlie MacCorry get into a fistfight over Laurie Mathison. Charlie is now a Texas Ranger. (Later on in the book, Charlie and Laurie are married.)

Heading south into New Mexico territory (the searchers had spent almost three years tracking leads at Northern forts and elsewhere), Amos and Martin find Lije Powers, who tells them about a Comanchero, Jamie Rosas. Led to Bluebonnet's camp by Rosas, the searchers find the chief has a white woman for a wife but, again, there is no sign of Debbie or Scar.

Three years later, Lije tells Martin and Amos he has seen Debbie with a chief called Yellow Buckle (later confirmed to be Scar). Amos tortures and kills a Comanche sniper to get information on Scar's campsite. As in the film, when the searchers confront Scar, they become aware of Debbie in the tepee. Soon after she comes to them by the creekbed and, although remembering her past, says that Scar is her father now. Amos does not try to shoot Debbie, as Ethan does in the film. He is wounded when the Comanches attack and she runs off.

In the attack on the Comanches, Martin and Amos join forces with Sol Clinton's Texas Rangers, a cavalry attachment led by Colonel Greenhill and a band of Indians called Tonkawas. Amos is shot and killed by a Comanche squaw whom he mistakens for Debbie. Having run away from Scar before the attack, Debbie is found by Martin. There is no mention in LeMay's novel on the fate of Scar.

The irony of Scar is that he is Ethan's equivalent in stature in the film, and also in prejudice, for it is a scar that Ethan carries in his own hate and fury. Both men seem cut out of the harsh land with its competing cultures of two races. Here the hatred Ethan feels for the Comanches who murdered his kinfolk is justified; however, Ford makes the message clear that his actions border on madness. Scar's cruelty toward white people is a reflection of having his own sons murdered by them. The director shows both races as being good and bad in their need to survive.

As Chief Scar, Henry Brandon has actually a small role, but his strong, deadly presence seems like a spectre that haunts the film. Unfortunately, the size of the part somewhat limits the actor's ability to express emotions as Wayne's Ethan. When Duke played the older cattleman in *Red River*, he was more tough than sensitive. In Ford's *She Wore a Yellow Ribbon*, Wayne (playing Nathan Brittles) was more sensitive than tough. The actor earned an Oscar nomination as Best Actor for his blend of toughness and sensitivity portraying Sergeant Stryker in Republic's 1949 war film *Sands of Iwo Jima* (Allan Dwan, director). But the culmination of his sensitivity and toughness was most remarkably presented in *The Searchers*.

Natalie Wood's role as Debbie is also relatively small, but the film's full pathos is revealed in her heartbreaking scenes; especially poignant is the moment where she tells Jeffrey Hunter's Martin that she remembers him and her childhood "from always." Wood's real-life sister Lana portrayed Debbie as a little girl with a great deal of poignancy as well. The scene where the child is placed outside the window to hide from the Indians, as her mother throws herself across the sill in tears, is difficult to watch. Tremendous tenderness is conveyed by Dorothy Jordan's Martha; her radiance is the very first touching thing about the movie when she opens the cabin door and steps outside to Max Steiner's truly beautiful music score.

As the secondary hero in the film, Hunter's part is developed with more clarity than Wayne's, although he is not as interesting. Martin's motive for finding Debbie is simpler because he just wants to bring her back home. Perhaps because of the clear-cut image of this character, fate deals him a clearer hand than the enigmatic Ethan when he and Vera Miles' Laurie are finally brought together. Miss Miles' sparkling and impish joy and frustration at Martin are delightful. Their performances are filled with youthful exuberance; their moments together and with Ken Curtis' Charlie McCorry are a comic respite from the grim search. The Fordian tomfoolery is enjoyable here, but it does have a tendency to prolong the actual search.

Ward Bond's crusty old Sam Clayton is the best of many performances from this wonderful character actor. A longtime stalwart in John Ford films, Bond made his first screen appearance in the director's 1929 football drama *Salute* (Fox). This movie featured Duke Wayne as well; the actors would become close friends, and they played football together at the University of Southern California.

In *The Searchers*, Bond played boisterously off everyone with such cussedness that he may have very well been imitating Ford. The scene that best conveys the director's own kindred spirit within Bond's character is when he remains perfectly quiet and stares right out at the viewer, realizing Ethan and Martha's love for each other; they briefly embrace behind him (an unspoken love that is as tender and gentle as the feeling between Marion and Shane).

Many in the supporting cast are members of the "John Ford Stock Company": Harry Carey, Jr., as Brad, John Qualen and Olive Carey (younger Carey's real mother) as his folks and Hank Worden as that dear fool, Mose Harper, who longs only for a rocking chair by the fireplace. Both Carey, Jr., and Worden had portrayed cowboys in *Red River*. John Wayne's own son Patrick was seen as the bumbling but dedicated young cavalry officer.

The film's most ironic feature is that old Mose, on his own solitary search for Debbie, finds her on both occasions for Martin and Ethan. When he located her the second time, the Comanches had journeyed back to near where the initial murder raid had begun. The racism felt by Scar and Ethan was also shared by others. Martin shoves Look off his bedroll, and Laurie attests that Ethan's desire to kill Debbie is because of her Indian taint. Such feelings were felt by white settlers when raids upon them began shortly before Texas become an independent country from Mexico in 1836. The Comanches felt threatened by the growing number of settlers competing with them for the land and buffalo.

An early leader of Texas, Sam Houston, attempted to bring peace between the races, but even more settlers came into the country when free land was given to them. In 1836, the Texas Rangers (comprised of white militia) began to combat the Indian raids. When Texas became a state in 1845, the Federal Government stepped in and deployed troops to a number of forts. A first attempt by the government to place the Indians on a reservation in 1855 failed, as the Comanches fought against the forced relocation.

Ten years later, after the Civil War, the government wanted to give the Comanches a wider territory, but Texas settlers refused to give up any land. As another ten years passed, more troops were allotted to force the Indians onto another reservation in the Indian territory of Oklahoma. The Comanches' might was dissipated in 1875 with the surrender of the great leader, Quanah Parker. A white woman, Cynthia Ann Parker, who was taken captive as a child, was Quanah's mother; his father was a Comanche, Peta Nocona. In 1889, the Oklahoma territory was opened by the government for the expansion of settlers; the land in question was located between the reservations of the Comanches and other Indian tribes. The famous landrush by settlers that followed was vividly presented in *Cimarron*.

The Searchers was filmed in the summer and fall of 1955; along with Monument Valley, Ford used locations in Canada (Edmonton, Alberta) and Colorado (Gunnison) for the buffalo and snow scenes (among others). One of the faults of the picture, however small, was that a few of the outdoor sequences appeared a little artificial, particularly the campfire scene as Ethan uses Martin as bait to smoke out Futterman. Nonetheless, Winton C. Hoch's color photography was outstanding — the stark beauty of Monument Valley conveyed perfectly the haunting sweep of the film. The big screen technique Vista-Vision gave added dimension to the images.

There were no Academy Award nominations for the film despite some of the best work done by longtime Ford collaborators cameraman Hoch, screenwriter Frank Nugent, assistant director Wingate Smith and executive producer Merian C. Cooper. The director's son Patrick received credit on *The Searchers* as associate producer.

The film's major financing came from entrepreneur Cornelius Vanderbilt Whitney, who had received a $20,000,000 inheritance in 1920. Among his varied interests were motion pictures, and his efforts included helping David O. Selznick with the production costs on *Gone With the Wind*. Credited as "A C.V. Whitney Picture," *The Searchers* represented his own realistic outlook on both a grim and humorous American West. The film cost $3,000,000; when it was released domestically by Warner Bros. in March '56 it made a handsome $4,900,000.

The Searchers received mixed reviews at the time. It was not until the 1970s that the film began to be called a masterpiece. By then a younger generation, growing up with a different set of values, more fully identified with the alienated outsider played by Wayne. The poetic beauty of John Ford's vast Western landscapes was appreciated from the beginning.

The perilous odyssey of Ethan Edwards, sadly, took longer. This role reaches the climax in a tremendous feeling of love when Ethan, finding he cannot harm his niece, tenderly cradles her in his arms. (There is some suggestion that Debbie may be his own daughter.) Ford tried in other films to grasp the tragedy of his heroes' strengths and weaknesses, and it is manifested to the fullest extent in this picture.

By the time Ethan holds his arm at the end (in fond remembrance of Harry Carey, Sr.'s stance from silent films), all his vulnerability and loneliness has been revealed. It is surely John Wayne's most touching characterization. He named his third son John Ethan Wayne, calling him Ethan after the part he played in *The Searchers*.

Reviews

Variety: "It's a Western in the grand scale — handsomely mounted and in the tradition of *Shane*.... The John Ford directorial stamp is unmistakable."

Library Journal: "The background scenes of ranch life and ranchers are authentic against scenery of great natural beauty. John Wayne's performance has a sturdy, haunting quality, and Ward Bond is excellent as Captain Clayton of the Texas Rangers who doubles as a preacher. Altogether an exciting and superior Western."

All gunfighters are lonely. They live in fear. They die without a dime, or a woman, or a friend.

BURT LANCASTER *as Wyatt Earp,*
to young Billy Clanton

Gunfight at the O.K. Corral

1957

Ready for trouble in Tombstone are (left to right) Kirk Douglas, Burt Lancaster, John Hudson, and DeForest Kelley.

GUNFIGHT AT THE O.K. CORRAL

A Hal B. Wallis Production. A Paramount Picture, 1957. Technicolor and VistaVision. Paramount Home Video. 122 minutes

Credits: John Sturges (Director); Hal B. Wallis (Producer); Paul Nathan (Associate Producer); Michael D. Moore (Assistant Director); Leon Uris (Screenplay); Charles Lang, Jr. (Photographer); Warren Low (Editor); Hal Pereira, Walter Tyler (Art Directors); Edith Head (Costumes); John P. Fulton (Special Effects); Dimitri Tiomkin (Music Score). Title song by Dimitri Tiomkin and Ned Washington; sung by Frankie Laine. Suggested by the magazine article *The Killer* by George Scullin.

Cast: Burt Lancaster (Wyatt Earp); Kirk Douglas (Doc Holliday); Rhonda Fleming (Laura Denbow); Jo Van Fleet (Kate Fisher); John Ireland (Johnny Ringo); Lyle Bettger (Ike Clanton); Frank Faylen (Cotton Wilson); Earl Holliman (Charles Bassett); Ted De Corsia (Shanghai Pierce); Dennis Hopper (Billy Clanton); Whit Bissell (John P. Clum); George Mathews (John Shanssey); John Hudson (Virgil Earp); DeForest Kelley (Morgan Earp); Martin Milner (James Earp); Kenneth Tobey (Bat Masterson); Lee Van Cleef (Ed Bailey); Joan Camden (Betty Earp); Olive Carey (Mrs. Clanton); Brian Hutton (Rick); Nelson Leigh (Mayor Kelley); Jack Elam (Tom McLowery); Don Castle (Drunken Cowboy); Mickey Simpson (Frank McLowery); Charles Herbert (Tommy Earp); Tony Merrill (Barber); Lee Roberts (Finn Clanton); Frank Carter (Hotel Clerk); Edward Ingram (Deputy); Bing Russell (Bartender); Henry Wills (Alby); Dorothy Abbott (Girl); William S. Meigs (Wayne); John Benson (Rig Driver); Richard J. Reeves (Foreman); John Maxwell (Merchant); Harry B. Mendoza (Cockeyed Frank Loving); Tony Joachim (Old Timer); Trude Wyler (Social Hall Guest); Robert C. Swan (Shaugnessy Man); Roger Creed (Deputy/Killer/Townsman); Bill Williams (Stuntman); Frank Hagney, Ethan Laidlaw (Bartenders); Paul Gary, Morgan Lane (Killers); Len Hendry, Gregg Martell, Dennis Moore (Cowboys); James Davies, Joe Forte, Max Power, Courtland Shepard (Card Players).

Synopsis

Three men on horseback ride across the prairie and into Fort Griffin, Texas. Entering the saloon, the trio are told to take off their guns (according to the town's law) by the owner, John Shanssey. The leader, Ed Bailey, is gunning for gambler Doc Holliday, who killed Bailey's brother. Although Shanssey states that the slain man was drunk and cheated at cards, Bailey wants revenge.

Doc, a heavy drinker wracked with a tubercular cough, is at the hotel with his mistress, Kate Fisher. She reminds him that his Southern family struggled so he could become a dentist (a practice now abandoned). Their relationship is filled with bitterness, but she fears for his life against Bailey.

Peace officer Wyatt Earp rides into town and is greeted by Marshal Cotton Wilson. Wyatt had sent word for Cotton to hold Ike Clanton, wanted for a dozen crimes; finding out he did not, Wyatt becomes angry enough to believe the old marshal has lost his nerve. Cotton, a lawman for 25 years, is disgruntled at having nothing but a room and a tin star to show for his time.

Upon asking Shanssey for help in picking up Ike's trail, Wyatt is advised to talk with Doc since he had played cards with both Ike and Johnny Ringo. On the way out of Shanssey's, Wyatt walks past Ed Bailey.

At the hotel, Wyatt tries to learn Ike's whereabouts from Doc. After informing the gambler that Bailey is hiding a derringer in his boot, Wyatt is taken aback when Doc refuses to trade information about Ike. Doc harbors a resentment against the Earps because Wyatt's brother Morgan, a lawman in Deadwood, once impounded some of the gambler's money.

Having gotten nowhere in his search for Clanton, Wyatt tells Shanssey that he will be leaving in the morning. Cotton is also at Shanssey's with his deputies, making sure Doc is unarmed. However, when Bailey reaches for his derringer, Doc reveals a knife and kills his adversary. Even though the act was in self-defense, Cotton arrests Doc and puts him under guard at the hotel. Kate's attempt to ask Wyatt for help proves futile, but Shanssey agrees to have a pair of saddled horses ready if needed.

With a lynch mob gathering, Kate again implores Wyatt to intervene. Although not approving of Doc's actions, Wyatt approves even less of lynch mobs and does help. He distracts the guard outside of Doc's room, then knocks him cold and frees Holliday. A signal is then passed to Kate, who sets fire to a nearby barn. The mob is distracted long enough for Doc and Kate to escape on the horses.

In Dodge City, Kansas, Wyatt is the town marshal. Deputy Charles Bassett lets Wyatt know that Doc and Kate are in town. Doc informs the marshal that he is flat broke, having paid Shanssey $5,000 apiece for the getaway horses. Realizing that Doc has to earn more money by playing cards, Wyatt allows him to stay in town after he promises no more killings.

When Wyatt learns from Charlie that a new lady in town, Laura Denbow, is gambling at the Long Branch Saloon, he makes her stop because female gamblers always seem to attract more trouble. Mayor Kelley brings to Wyatt's

Kirk Douglas (left) and Burt Lancaster.

attention Laura's fine reputation, but the marshal stands firm. When a drunken cowboy tries to intervene, Wyatt uses the incident as an excuse to put Laura in jail.

Learning of Laura's predicament from the mayor, Doc jovially goes to her rescue. He first persuades Charlie that she should be released, and even Wyatt relents after Doc shares the news that cattleman Shanghai Pierce has put a $1,000 bounty on the lawman's head. Both Doc and Mayor Kelley join Laura at a gaming table in an adjoining room to the main saloon (as is Wyatt's order). Kate is standing by getting drunk and feeling neglected.

Word reaches Wyatt that a neighboring town's bank has been robbed, and that the outlaws are heading his way. With his other deputies away on business with lawman Bat Masterson, Wyatt deputizes Doc to hunt down the outlaws with him.

Making camp that night, Doc reveals that he plans on saving Wyatt's life in order to settle his past obligations to the marshal. The three outlaws do try to kill Wyatt as he sleeps, but he and Doc are able to kill them instead. Back in town, Doc's coughing has gotten worse; looking for Kate to help him, he is told by Charlie that she has left their hotel.

Aware that Laura rides out each morning to the country, Wyatt follows her. Having a lame horse, she rides behind him on his mount back into town.

Collecting the firearms from Pierce's arriving cowboys at the cattle yards, Charlie reluctantly tells Doc that Kate has taken up with Johnny Ringo. Later on, Doc finds her at Ringo's hotel; the two men almost shoot it out over her, but the gambler remembers his promise to Wyatt. Ringo then humiliates Doc by throwing a glass of whiskey in his face.

That same evening, Wyatt and Laura take a buggy ride together into the country. They soon embrace and kiss, realizing they are in love.

Meanwhile, Shanghai Pierce is in town with Ringo and his cowboys on a drunken shooting spree. Wyatt returns and single-handedly tries to restore peace. Ringo takes aim at Wyatt, but Doc comes to the rescue and shoots Ringo in the arm. The rowdy bunch are then locked up for the night. Doc now feels that any past debts to the marshal are paid.

Wyatt tells Doc that he is giving up being a lawman to marry Laura and start a ranch in California. Doc turns Kate away when she wants to come back to him. Wyatt's life with Laura is threatened when he receives word from brother Virgil that his help is needed in Tombstone, Arizona. Laura does not want Wyatt to be a lawman, fearful that he will be killed. Wyatt rides away from her, yet only to end the trouble in Tombstone. Doc joins Wyatt on the trail.

In Tombstone, Wyatt drops Doc off at the Alhambra Saloon before joining his brothers Virgil, Morgan and James and Virgil's wife and son. Virgil is the town marshal. Wyatt is told the trouble is with old nemesis Ike Clanton. Having put together a gang of gunfighters, Ike is rustling cattle. Cotton Wilson, now the county sheriff, is owned by Clanton.

Ike wants to ship his stolen herd through Tombstone and has Cotton offer Wyatt a $20,000 bribe. Wyatt refuses. The carrying of firearms in town is forbidden.

Ike rides into Tombstone with his gang, which includes Ringo, and they plan on keeping their guns to attend a show by entertainer Eddie Foy. Wyatt disarms Ike; Virgil, Morgan, James and the Citizen's Committee, headed by John P. Clum, help force Clanton and his gang out of town.

Arriving on the stage is Kate, taking up once again with Ringo. At the saloon, Ringo goads Doc into meeting him in the street for a gunfight. On the way, Doc is stopped by Virgil, who says that his friendship with Wyatt is the worst thing to happen since he is a noted killer.

Wyatt visits Doc in his hotel room upon learning that the gambler plans to leave town. Somewhat disheartened, Wyatt states that he is sorry they both will not be together to end the trouble with the Clanton gang.

When Ike's young brother, Billy, is brought drunk into jail by Morgan, Wyatt carries him back to the Clanton Ranch. Wyatt shows understanding since the younger Clanton looks up to his older brothers Ike and Finn as the lawman looked up to his own. Billy's mother is upset that he will end up shot down as a rustler like his father. Ike rides up with Cotton and is set to draw his gun on the unarmed lawman until Wyatt reveals his new appointment as United States Marshal. Eager to deal with Wyatt, Ike is told simply to drive his stolen cattle back to Mexico.

Unable to do anything about Wyatt's appointment, Ike plans then with his gang (Kate is also present) to kill the lawman as he makes his nightly rounds in Tombstone. The entire gang knows this will force the other Earps into a personal vendetta because of a sense of family pride.

That night, young James, anxious to return to his own sweetheart in California, takes Wyatt's place to make the rounds. He is ambushed and gunned down in the street by the Clanton Gang, who believed he was Wyatt in the darkness. Doc urges Wyatt not to make it a personal fight with the outlaws since it is exactly what they crave.

Doc forces Kate to reveal all the participants in the murder. As he prepares to strike her, Doc is overcome by his coughing and loses consciousness. Kate stays with him.

Billy Clanton comes into town to let Wyatt know he had no part in James' death, and that Ike will meet the Earps at sunup at the O.K. Corral for a showdown. With Ike will be Finn, Ringo, the McLowery Brothers (Tom and Frank) and Billy, who, like Wyatt, feels a bond with his own brothers.

Virgil's wife Betty tries in vain to persuade the Earp Brothers not to put foolish pride before their responsibility as lawmen and to ask John Clum for help. Wyatt walks down to the O.K. Corral, now quiet, and lights a lantern on a wagon as he reflects on the bitter turn of events. He then goes to Doc's room to plead with his friend for help, but the gambler is still unconscious. Kate believes that Doc is dying.

At sunup, Mrs. Clanton can only watch in despair as her sons ride with their gang into Tombstone. Doc is awake. Despite Kate's concern, he joins Wyatt in his room and together they meet Virgil and Morgan waiting outside. The four men are armed as they walk side by side down the street toward the Corral.

Waiting there with guns ready are the outlaws. Watching their horses is Cotton Wilson. In the ensuing gunfight, Finn Clanton wounds Morgan Earp. Protecting Morgan from further injury, Doc Holliday kills Finn. Wyatt manages to shoot the still-lit lantern, setting the wagon on fire. Cotton, wanting no part of the gunplay, tries to ride off but is gunned down by Ike. With the wagon blazing away, Frank McLowery catches fire and falls dead; his brother

Tom rushes after Wyatt, who cuts him down. Running to join Wyatt, Virgil Earp is wounded by Ike. Protecting his injured brother, Wyatt kills Ike. Billy Clanton wounds Doc slightly, but in turn is wounded by Wyatt. Doc shoots down Johnny Ringo. Wyatt, chasing after Billy, does not want to kill him; however, Doc is forced to in order to save his friend. Standing over young Billy's body, Wyatt drops his gun, then his badge.

Afterwards, in the Alhambra, Wyatt tells Doc that Morgan and Virgil will live. He also tells Doc that he is going to California to try to join Laura. Doc is urged to seek help for his cough. As Doc Holliday sits down to play cards, Wyatt Earp rides out of Tombstone.

In 1931, Stuart N. Lake wrote his famous biography *Wyatt Earp: Frontier Marshal*. A film called *Law and Order* (directed by Edward Cahn) was released the following year by Universal. Based not on Lake's book but on a novel by W.R. Burnett, this early sound film set fictitiously yet with grim forbearance the mystique surrounding the resolute Earp persona and the most celebrated gunfight in Western history. Walter Huston played a character based on Earp named Saint Johnson. In '34, Lake's book was the source for Fox's *Frontier Marshal* (directed by Lew Seiler), with George O'Brien playing Michael Wyatt, a character similar to the famed lawman. Having obtained the rights to Lake's biography, Fox remade this last film in 1939, using the same title (but with director Allan Dwan). The hero, as played by Randolph Scott, was actually called Wyatt Earp. In '46, 20th Century–Fox remade the film as *My Darling Clementine* (even using incidents from the previous picture but now to more memorable effect). The title refers to the film's gentle heroine.

My Darling Clementine is a charming piece of Americana. Director John Ford gave to his low-keyed Western his customary sentiment and simplicity of character (only Victor Mature's Doc Holliday is an enigma, seemingly caught between being good or bad, just as the feared gunman was supposed to have been). The tender romance between Henry Fonda's Wyatt Earp and Cathy Downs' Clementine Carter is the sort of homespun touch Ford indulged in so well; probably for this reason more than any other, admirers of the film cite it as the best of the Wyatt Earp movies. But there is one film which may just surpass it for revealing the Earp legend in its full mythic scope.

In 1957, 11 years after John Ford's superb film, Paramount released the equally superb *Gunfight at the O.K. Corral*. Producer Hal B. Wallis and director John Sturges brilliantly conveyed a storybook Western with historical overtones. *My Darling Clementine* did as well; yet the leisurely pace and spartan look of this earlier classic now gave way to even more riveting suspense, spectacular action and richer details. In *Clementine*, you would never guess that its little town of Tombstone was actually a major community in the Old West (with a population of nearly 10,000 by 1881) because of a big silver strike. In *Gunfight*, you know that its Tombstone is booming. (Not mentioned in either film is the fact that silver was discovered in the nearby Arizona hills by prospector Ed Schieffelin in 1877, two years before Wyatt Earp rode into town.)

The large-scale production values of *Gunfight at the O.K. Corral* are typical of successful producer Hal B. Wallis. His reign with Warner Bros. during the 1930s and early '40s is legendary; among the many classic films he helped produce were 1938's *The Adventures of Robin Hood* (Michael Curtiz and William Keighley, directors); 1942's *Yankee Doodle Dandy*; and 1943's *Casablanca* (again with director Curtiz). Among Wallis' Westerns for the studio (all with Curtiz) were 1939's *Dodge City* and 1940's *Virginia City* and *Santa Fe Trail*. In '44, Wallis joined Paramount and the list of films he produced with them was also impressive. He was instrumental in making movie stars of both Burt Lancaster and Kirk Douglas when they were brought to Hollywood in 1946.

Outstanding craftsmen who worked with Hal Wallis on *Gunfight* were cinematographer Charles Lang, Jr.; art directors Hal Pereira and Walter Tyler; and editor Warren Low. But equal credit for the film's panoramic sweep must go to Sturges, whose contributions as a director enhanced the wide screen format then in vogue. This film used to breathtaking effect the same Technicolor and VistaVision processes that Ford's *The Searchers* did the year before. Hence, *Gunfight*'s backgrounds often seemed like magnificent paintings and its action like a pulsating choreographed ballad. Frankie Laine's haunting rendition of Dimitri Tiomkin and Ned Washington's title song was actually heard from time to time as a stirring ballad (reminiscent of the duo's *High Noon*), and was a memorable complement to Sturges' majestic direction.

Sturges began his film career with RKO-Radio Pictures in the early 1930s, doing technical jobs. It was not until he entered the Army Air Corps that he began directing; between 1942–45, he worked on several dozen documentaries in this capacity. His first feature film as a director was Columbia's drama *The Man Who Dared* (1946). Under a Columbia contract, Sturges directed his first Western, *The Walking Hills* starring Randolph Scott, in 1949. Moving over to Metro-Goldwin-Mayer, his initial Western as a director was 1953's *Escape from Fort Bravo* (with William Holden). Both of these Westerns were effective but not memorable. However, in 1955, Sturges made for MGM the contemporary Western *Bad Day at Black Rock*, for which he used the wide screen format to heighten the tension. It earned him a Directors Guild of America Award as well as an Academy Award nomination for Best Director. *Gunfight at the O.K. Corral* was his first film for Paramount.

The studio had made a film on the Wyatt Earp legend in '42 called *Tombstone, the Town Too Tough to Die* (William McGann, director; with Richard Dix portraying Earp). In '55, Joel McCrea played Wyatt in Allied Artists' *Wichita* (Jacques Tourneur, director). This film had the distinction of having Earp biographer, Stuart Lake, as technical advisor. For 57's *Gunfight*, its screenwriter Leon Uris drew his inspiration not from Lake's book but from a 1954 *Holiday Magazine* article (*The Killer*) by George Scullin.

Quoting dialogue from Lake's biography, *The Killer* was a historical profile of John "Doc" Holliday, born to an aristocratic Southern family in 1850. Devastated by the Civil War, the family had to mortgage their plantation to put Holliday through dental school in Baltimore, Maryland. The magazine article relates that Holliday, stricken with consumption, and having killed two innocent people in a rage, went West. The film does depict Doc's tubercular condition, as does *My Darling Clementine* and other versions, although the Ford film depicted him as a surgeon rather than a dentist. According to Scullin, Holliday practiced dentistry in Texas before turning to card playing and sometimes killing when the gambling became heated.

In 1877, wrote Scullin, Doc took up with a local madam, Kate Fisher, in Fort Griffin (*Gunfight* soft-pedals her profession). The writer mentions that Holliday's first meeting with Wyatt Earp was in this town (the film's opening sequence takes place here, but refers to an initial meeting ten years earlier when Doc pulled Wyatt's tooth). Both the magazine article and film highlight Doc's killing of Ed Bailey (the article contends that it was over a card game). Kate's subsequent diversion of the lynch mob was factually based; the film to the contrary, Wyatt was not involved.

As in the film, Doc and Kate wound up in Dodge City (Scullin sets the date as 1878). The town's marshal was Wyatt Earp. The movie's confrontation between Wyatt and cattleman Shanghai Pierce happened at another time. Doc did help Wyatt against a bunch of rowdy cowboys, but the article stipulates that they were led by Tobe Driskill and Ed Morrison, not Pierce. Holliday did wound a cowboy here, but not the film's Johnny Ringo.

Scullin's tale continued with Wyatt reunited with his brothers Virgil, Morgan and James in Tombstone. Doc had joined Wyatt on the trail. Their conflict with a gang of outlaws culminated in the O.K. Corral gunfight on October 26, 1881 (none of the article's dates are mentioned in the film).

Sturges' *Gunfight*, like Ford's *Clementine*, fabricates the facts of the actual gunfight; the film battles are longer (Ford even kills off Doc). Scullin describes the gunplay, as does Stuart Lake, with great accuracy—17 shots were fired from each camp in 30 seconds. Morgan and Virgil were wounded, and Tom and Frank McLowery as well as Billy Clanton were killed. Ike Clanton ran away along with two others, Billy Claiborne and Wes Fuller. Johnny Ringo and Phineas Clanton (Finn in the film) were part of the outlaw gang, but they were not involved at the O.K. Corral.

While *Gunfight at the O.K. Corral* ended with the deadly shootout, its aftermath is mentioned by both Scullin and Lake. Other members of the outlaw gang crippled Virgil and murdered Morgan later on, and Wyatt and Doc led a posse against the assassins. Lake further mentions the mysterious death of Ringo (found shot) and the unrelated killing of Ike (killed while rustling cattle). Both writers tell of Doc's dying of tuberculosis at 35. Wyatt lived until 1929.

Wyatt Earp was born in 1848. Legend has it that after arresting gunman Ben Thompson in Ellsworth, Kansas, in '73, he was offered the job of deputy marshal in the Kansas cow town of Wichita. In 1876, Wyatt became the chief deputy in Dodge City, perhaps the most famous cow town of them all. Another legendary lawman, Bartholomew "Bat" Masterson, was one of his deputies for a time. He was replaced by Bat's brother Ed until the latter was killed and Wyatt became town marshal. Bat was county sheriff at the time. Wyatt's fearlessness as a lawman was already well-established when he moved on to Tombstone in 1879 with his brothers James, Virgil and Morgan to take advantage of the mining market opportunities. Wyatt was a faro dealer and part-owner of the Oriental Saloon. By the time of the gunfight at the O.K. Corral in '81, Virgil was town marshal with Wyatt, Morgan and Doc Holliday his deputies.

Director Sturges reconstructed his fanciful yet sensational gunfight at a site called Old Tucson, Arizona, and it took four days to shoot. Other Arizona locations included Phoenix and Tombstone. Ironically, the gunfight was depicted with far more accuracy in the director's less successful 1967 Western *Hour of the Gun*. This sequel of sorts was for United Artists, and it starred James Garner as Wyatt, Jason Robards as Doc and Robert Ryan as Ike. Also produced by Sturges, it was a somber account of the aftermath of the gunfight with an interesting mix of fact and fiction.

Equally interesting were the vivid depictions of the gunfight and its aftermath in 1993's *Tombstone* (Buena Vista; George P. Cosmatos, director) and 1994's *Wyatt Earp* (Warner Bros.; Lawrence Kasdan, director). *Tombstone* cast Kurt Russell as Wyatt and Val Kilmer as Doc while *Wyatt Earp* had Kevin Costner and Dennis Quaid in those roles. For these two films, as well as *Hour of the Gun* and *My Darling Clementine*, electric performances as Earp and Holliday were given by one and all. Yet none seemed as powerful as Burt Lancaster and Kirk Douglas, whose virility overshadowed the others.

Hal Wallis brought Douglas and Lancaster to films from the Broadway stage — in 1945, Kirk was in the fantasy drama *The Wind Is Ninety* and Burt was in the war drama *A Sound of Hunting*. Their initial films for Wallis at Paramount were both dramas — Kirk in 1946's *The Strange Love of Martha Ivers*

(Lewis Milestone, director), Burt in 1947's *Desert Fury* (Lewis Allen, director). However, Lancaster had already become an overnight star via Universal's 1946 gangster classic *The Killers* (Robert Siodmak, director). Douglas reached full stardom and earned his first Oscar nomination for Best Actor with Stanley Kramer's boxing classic *Champion* (1949). In the interim between these films, the actors co-starred for Wallis and Paramount in 1948's drama *I Walk Alone* (Byron Haskin, director).

In 1951, both actors made their first Western. Lancaster's was *Vengeance Valley* (MGM; director, Richard Thorpe) while Douglas' was *Along the Great Divide* (Warner Bros.; director, Raoul Walsh). In '52, Kirk was in Howard Hawks' Western adventure *The Big Sky*; he received a second Academy Award nomination that same year for Vincente Minnelli's drama *The Bad and the Beautiful*. In '53, Burt received his first Oscar nomination for Best Actor in Fred Zinnemann's much-heralded *From Here to Eternity* (co-starring Montgomery Clift).

Lancaster made three Westerns in a row for United Artists and his own production company (which he formed in '48 with producer Harold Hecht) — 1954's *Apache* and *Vera Cruz* (both for director Robert Aldrich) and 1955's *The Kentuckian* (which Burt also directed). In 1955, Douglas made a pair of Westerns — Universal's *Man Without a Star* (director, King Vidor) and his initial venture for his own production outfit, *The Indian Fighter* (director, Andre de Toth).

Nineteen fifty-six saw Kirk realize a third Oscar nomination for MGM's drama, *Lust for Life* (again with director Minnelli); Burt realized his company's biggest box office hit with the drama, *Trapeze* (director, Carol Reed). Undeniably, Douglas and Lancaster were major filmmakers in their own right by this time.

As actors, they were renowned for their vitality yet sensitivity in a wide assortment of roles. Wallis knew their strengths would be a perfect match for *Gunfight at the O.K. Corral*. At first Lancaster was reluctant to star in the Western until the producer allowed him to play in Paramount's '56 drama, *The Rainmaker* (Joseph Anthony, director). With *Gunfight*, Burt was fulfilling his original contract with Hal Wallis; Kirk had gotten out of his contract after *I Walk Alone*. Lancaster and Douglas were terrific in *Gunfight* — their own legendary status reflected memorably the stature of their respective Wyatt Earp and Doc Holliday. Somewhat minimized was the inherent violence of the actual gunmen. The violence was exploited by the later films *Tombstone* and *Wyatt Earp*.

In *Gunfight at the O.K. Corral*, John Ireland, who played Billy Clanton in *My Darling Clementine*, was now the enigmatic Johnny Ringo, selling his gun to the highest bidder. Ireland was a badman against Lancaster in *Vengeance*

Valley (Ireland's equally bad brother in that film was Hugh O'Brian, later television's own Wyatt Earp). Lyle Bettger was the film's Ike Clanton, while Lee Van Cleef was Ed Bailey and Jack Elam was Tom McLowery. These sturdy actors always made unforgettable villains. Jo Van Fleet's fiery dramatics as Kate Fisher matched Douglas' breath for breath. Rhonda Fleming radiated dignity and charm as Laura Denbow; this mystery lady was actually fictitious. So was Cotton Wilson, played by the fine character actor Frank Faylen. (Historically, there was a county sheriff in Tombstone, Johnny Behan, who opposed the Earps. Among the ladies in Wyatt's life was an actress, Josephine Sarah Marcus; they were married for 45 years.)

Equally fine were actors John Hudson and DeForest Kelley in short but unforgettable roles as Virgil and Morgan Earp. Among the talented newcomers appearing in the film were Dennis Hopper as Billy Clanton, Earl Holliman as Charles Bassett and Martin Milner as James Earp. Both *Gunfight* and *Clementine* made James the youngest of the Earps, when in truth he was Wyatt's older brother and lived until 1926.

For all the elaborations on the controversial O.K. Corral showdown, the films which have explored the Wyatt Earp legend have done so in grand style. Yet *Gunfight at the O.K. Corral* remains the most slickly produced film to convey the folklore tinged with historical fact. The film was nominated for a pair of Academy Awards — Editing (Warren Low) and Sound (George Dutton). The sounds of the gunplay seem to explode right out at you, and the film, although a bit overlong, is paced with utmost precision. But Peter Taylor won for editing the war film *The Bridge on the River Kwai* (Columbia; David Lean, director), and sound man George Groves won the other Oscar for the drama *Sayonara* (Joshua Logan, director).

So intent was Hal Wallis on having Kirk Douglas and Burt Lancaster for *Gunfight at the O.K. Corral* that he was forced to pay them many times what he had when they first started out. After the Western's May '57 release, and the big domestic earnings of $4,700,000, Wallis knew the gamble was worth it.

Reviews

Newsweek: "Richly furnished and lovingly photographed, *Gunfight* fairly swims in sumptuous color; the interiors have a rich glow to them, and the landscapes are dreamlike."

National Parent-Teacher: "The legend of Wyatt Earp and Doc Holliday has taken on artistry in this beautifully produced Western. Burt Lancaster is cast as Wyatt Earp in a heroic, larger-than-life role. Doc Holliday, brilliantly acted by Kirk Douglas, is an intense and lonely person."

Here on these ramparts, you have bought a price-
less ten days of time for Houston. You have bled
the enemy army. You are brave and noble soldiers.

LAURENCE HARVEY *as Colonel William Barret Travis,*
to all the Alamo defenders

The Alamo

1960

Left to right: Richard Widmark, John Wayne, and Laurence Harvey.

THE ALAMO

A Batjac Production. Released by United Artists, 1960. Technicolor. Todd-AO. MGM/UA Home Video. 202 minutes.

Credits: John Wayne (Director and Producer); James Edward Grant (Associate Producer and Screenplay); Robert E. Relyea, Robert Saunders (Assistant Directors); Cliff Lyons (Second Unit Director); William H. Clothier (Photographer); Stuart Gilmore (Editor); Alfred Ybarra (Art Director); Victor Gangelin (Set Decorator); Frank Beetson, Ann Peck (Costumes); Web Overlander (Makeup); Lee Zavitz (Special Effects); Dimitri Tiomkin (Music); Paul Francis Webster (Lyrics). Songs: "The Green Leaves of Summer," "Tennessee Babe," "Here's to the Ladies."

Cast: John Wayne (Colonel David Crockett); Richard Widmark (Colonel James Bowie); Laurence Harvey (Colonel William Barret Travis); Richard Boone (General Sam Houston); Frankie Avalon (Smitty); Patrick Wayne (Captain James Bonham); Linda Cristal (Flaca); Joan O'Brien (Mrs. Dickinson); Chill Wills (Beekeeper); Joseph Calleia (Juan Seguin); Ken Curtis (Captain Dickinson); Carlos Arruza (Lieutenant Reyes); Jester Hairston (Jethro); Veda Ann Borg (Blind Nell); John Dierkes (Jocko Robertson); Denver Pyle (Gambler); Aissa Wayne (Lisa Dickinson); Hank Worden (Parson); Bill Henry (Dr. Sutherland); Bill Daniel (Colonel Neill); Wesley Lau (Emil); Chuck Roberson, Rudy Robbins (Tennesseans); Guinn Williams (Lieutenant Finn); Olive Carey (Mrs. Dennison); Ruben Padilla (Santa Anna); Jack Pennick (Lightfoot).

Synopsis

In 1836, Texas is under the flag of Mexico. All who live there are Mexican citizens. Santa Anna, the Mexican generalissimo, is forcing all to bend before his oppressive rule.

Leading a group of rebels is General Sam Houston, holding an officers' meeting in San Antonio. One officer, Colonel James Bowie, is unable to attend, having gotten drunk after winning a battle. Bowie has a big stake in Texas, having married into Mexican aristocracy. Houston entrusts William Barret Travis with a new commission as colonel and to keep Santa Anna's forces at bay while the general raises an army. Travis leads 27 regular soldiers; Bowie's 100 volunteers are also under his command.

After Houston's departure, Travis orders Bowie's men into an old mission called the Alamo, now being used as a fort. Bowie feels that it is futile to try to secure the dilapidated church against Santa Anna's approaching army of 7,000 troops, but Travis does not agree. There is a growing antagonism between the two men.

When San Antonio's mayor, Juan Seguin, brings word to Travis that the Mexican forces are closer than anticipated, the Alamo commander dismisses this as third hand news and unreliable. This action further infuriates Bowie, who thinks Travis is a fool. The rudeness to Seguin surprises Travis' own second in command, Captain Dickinson, whose wife Sue and daughter Lisa are among the Alamo's women and children.

Colonel David Crockett and a feisty group of 23 fellow Tennesseans ride into San Antonio for hunting and partying. At the local cantina that night, Crockett meets Travis. At first Travis takes offense at the wild antics of the Tennesseans, but he is soon humbled by Crockett's eloquent rhetoric on the future plans to make Texas into a Republic.

While out on a stroll that evening, Davy comes across a man and a woman in a heated argument. The woman, named Flaca, is being forced into a loveless marriage with the man in order to have her confiscated family property returned to her by Santa Anna. When Davy offers her his help, the other man has a gang of cutthroats chase him down. With Jim Bowie's unexpected help, the gang is beaten and driven off.

Jim informs Davy that the gang's leader is a local merchant named Emil. As the two new friends get better acquainted at the cantina, Jim mentions to Davy that his wife and children were sent North because of the impending Mexican attack. The woman from earlier on arrives to tell Davy that Emil has hidden gunpowder in a nearby church's basement.

Accompanied by Tennesseans Smitty, Parson, Beekeeper and Bowie, Crockett not only finds the gunpowder but rifles as well. When they are confronted by an armed Emil, Davy kills him with Bowie's knife. Later, Davy tells Flaca about the killing. They are attracted to each other.

The following day, as Santa Anna's soldiers move closer to San Antonio, Davy, Jim, Smitty and Beekeeper take the powder and weapons to the Alamo. Travis informs Bowie and Crockett that Colonel Fannin will be coming from Goliad with additional troops to enforce their garrison. Bowie is angry that Travis wants him to build up the men's morale by lying to them about the actual number of reinforcements. Trying to find a way to get his men to fight with Travis, Crockett has Flaca write a letter in Spanish and then pretends it is a letter from Santa Anna threatening the Tennesseans. Although Davy later admits it is a ruse, his comrades still decide to join up with Travis.

While on a ride in the country with Flaca, Davy tells her about the purpose brought back into his life by fighting against an injustice. As they are now seemingly in love, Davy sends Flaca away to safety.

As Crockett and his men move into the Alamo, Bowie believes their fight against Santa Anna would be better served by using hit-and-run tactics. The Mexican soldiers begin entering San Antonio and the townspeople hide in fear. When an enemy rider reads a declaration against the rebels in the Alamo, Travis answers with a cannon blast.

Awaiting Santa Anna's main forces, 2,000 Mexican troops position themselves within sight of the fort. Beekeeper wonders if Davy has taken on too much. When Bowie decides to take his men out, Travis brands him a traitor.

Captain James Bonham arrives from Goliad with news that Fannin is on his way, but reluctantly lies to Bowie, on Travis' orders, that it is with 1,000 men instead of really 500. Bowie decides then to stay and wait for Fannin. A scout, Lieutenant Finn, reports that the Mexicans have a mammoth cannon.

That night, Bowie and Crockett sneak off to destroy the cannon. Although the mission is successful, Captain Dickinson is forced to hold back the enemy, thereby risking more lives. Returning to the fort, young Smitty saves Bowie's life when a horse they had doubled up on folds under them.

Travis threatens to arrest him if he continues to act without orders. Jim then decides to take his men out at daybreak. The Alamo commander informs Crockett that he intends to buy every bit of time for Houston. Davy tries to get Jim drunk in order to change his mind about leaving.

The ploy works, but Jim is embarrassed when confronted by Smitty, who looks up to him. Jim wallops Davy for not letting him make up his own mind about staying. Later, Bowie receives from Juan Seguin some badly needed reinforcements from the Texas town of Gonzales.

Little Lisa Dickinson's birthday party is celebrated by all in the Alamo. This pleasant occasion brings a bit of comfort to the fort's defenders, who momentarily forget the threat outside their walls.

Jim receives a message that his wife has died from a plague. Davy shows immediate sympathy for his distraught friend. Tainted meat causes mild dysentery among the fort's women and children. Travis decides to raid the enemy camp for cattle. Under cover of darkness, a group of the Alamo men sneak into the camp and at sunrise drive the cattle into the fort. In the interim, Smitty is sent with a plea to General Houston. Travis executes a brilliant stratagem, using riflemen to drive back the angry Mexican soldiers.

Santa Anna arrives with his main forces; a declaration is dispatched that the Alamo's women and children can be safely evacuated. But Sue Dickinson refuses to go. Lieutenant Finn, who has no family, graciously says goodbye to another mother. One of Bowie's men, Jocko, finds it hard to leave his blind wife and their children, but she tells him to stay with his comrades. Immediately after the evacuation, the siege of the Alamo begins in full force.

In the first attack, the fort's defenders kill many of the enemy as they try to storm the walls. The parson is mortally wounded by a cannon blast; Bowie is hit in the leg trying to help him. The fallen Mexicans are allowed to receive care by their women and fellow soldiers. Crockett, shaken by the parson's death, says a prayer over him for all his men. Dickinson reports that 28 of their comrades were killed in the initial fusillade. Travis' hopes that Fannin will shortly arrive are dashed when Captain Bonham returns with the news that the 500 reinforcements have been ambushed and murdered.

Crockett and Bowie agree now is the time to take their men out of the Alamo. As they all ride toward the gates, Travis praises them for their gallant efforts, proclaiming that he must stay with his command. Bowie, in the lead, gets off his horse and stands beside Travis, as does his Negro servant Jethro and then all his volunteers. They are joined by Crockett and his Tennesseans.

Smitty rides into Houston's camp with his message about the dire predicament at the Alamo. The young man then rides out, not stopping for rest nor food. Still organizing his army, Sam Houston hopes that Texas will remember the Alamo's brave sacrifice as 185 comrades buy this precious time with their lives.

On the eve of the final attack, Dickinson spends time with his wife and child. The defenders reflect on their fate, some with religious fervor. Bowie gives Jethro his freedom, and the old man decides to stay on at the Alamo.

At dawn, Santa Anna's entire army marches into position and attacks the fort. Although their defense is valiant, the defenders are soon overwhelmed as the enemy troops breach the walls. Bowie, because of his leg injury, is carried into the chapel by his comrades. Finn is killed with a sword thrust but takes two of the enemy with him. Travis, trying to secure a cannon, is forced to fight with his sword; he slays three Mexican soldiers before he is shot and killed. Dickinson is also shot and falls over a wooden barricade. Bonham shoots one enemy and kills another with his sword before being cut down by a Mexican rider's own sword. Beekeeper is also run through with a sword.

Crockett, who is trying to hold the Alamo's weakest defense, disables two enemy horsemen, but is forced back by the surge of enemy riders. He is speared into a door by a Mexican soldier; as he dies, Crockett throws a torch into the munitions room, causing a massive explosion. Bowie fights in the chapel with all the weapons in his grasp, including his fabled knife; Jethro throws his own body across Bowie's and both men are bayoneted to death. Every patriot is killed. The Alamo doctor is the last defender to die.

Mrs. Dickinson, her daughter and a Negro servant boy are the only survivors of the Alamo. Santa Anna has his troops stand at attention as the three

The death of Davy Crockett (John Wayne) at the Alamo.

survivors are allowed to pass safely by. Smitty has returned. On the crest of a hill overlooking the carnage, he is joined by the woman and children.

In the four years between John Ford's *The Searchers* and John Wayne's *The Alamo*, there seemed to be no end to the Westerns being made for the cinema and television. The motion picture market often thought in epic terms so as to compete with the booming television market. Big cinematic Westerns included 1956's *Giant* (Warner Bros.; director, George Stevens); 1958's *The Big Country* (United Artists; director, William Wyler); and 1960's remake of *Cimarron* (MGM; director, Anthony Mann). Smaller budgeted but impressive Westerns abounded, including Anthony Mann's *The Tin Star* (1957) and Gordon Douglas' *Yellowstone Kelly* (1959).

The latter film's star, Clint Walker, was also well known at the time for ABC's Western television series *Cheyenne*. CBS' *Gunsmoke* was the highest rated television program from the beginning of the 1957 season through 1961. In the 1958/59 television season, seven of the top ten programs were Westerns. NBC's *Bonanza* premiered in the Fall '59 season, and was listed in the top 25 shows by the following year.

Nineteen fifty-nine was a busy year for Duke Wayne. Not only was he producing, directing and starring in *The Alamo* for his own Batjac Productions and United Artists (for release in '60), but he was in a pair of Westerns for his two favorite directors, John Ford and Howard Hawks. For Ford, Wayne was in United Artists' *The Horse Soldiers*; and for Hawks, he starred in Warner Bros.' *Rio Bravo*. Wayne and Hawks felt that *Rio Bravo* was their answer to *High Noon*, a film they disagreed with strongly because the marshal throws down his badge at the end. They also objected to that marshal's isolating himself from an old drunk and a teenager. In *Rio Bravo*, Wayne's sheriff, John T. Chance, is a professional in the mold of Gary Cooper's lawman, but he is forced to accept help from a drunk, an elderly cripple and a very young man.

Many Western films tried to humanize their protagonists in an exciting frontier background in order to adhere to the Hollywood interpretation of the Old West. This was also true of television Westerns although the production values, for the most part, were not as costly, and the violence was toned down as compared to feature films. *The Alamo* did not waver from its exciting frontier fortitude nor in its spirited interpreting of the historical perspective and horrific violence of the immortal fight for liberty. The Daughters of the Republic of Texas, who are responsible for the preservation of the historic Alamo in San Antonio, Texas, state that 189 patriots withstood for 13 days an assault by eventually 4,000 Mexican troops (not the 7,000 ascribed to in the film).

Despite the criticism levelled at the film after its October 1960 release — for being too loud, too preachy, too long — it is a magnificent tribute to freedom and to the martyred heroes of the Alamo.

John Wayne had dreamed of filming the story of the Alamo throughout the 1950s. While under contract to Republic Pictures' head Herbert Yates, Wayne tried to get it made with that studio. Yates, while interested in the idea, was against the location filming and big budget that Duke felt the project deserved. Wayne then broke his contract with Republic, and Yates was upset enough to make his own Alamo film in '55 called *The Last Command* (director, Frank Lloyd). Less ambitious although a strong dramatization of the tragic siege (second unit director William Witney handled much of the Alamo battle), this picture starred Sterling Hayden as James Bowie, Arthur Hunnicutt as Davy Crockett and Richard Carlson as William Travis. (Republic had also made a brief pilgrimage to the Alamo in a handsome 1939 biography of Sam Houston, *Man of Conquest,* directed by George Nicholls, Jr., with Richard Dix portraying the great Texas leader. In this account, Victor Jory was Travis, Robert Barrat was Crockett and Robert Armstrong was Bowie.)

Paramount and Warner Bros. supposedly were interested in Wayne's *Alamo* project but only if he would star and not direct. They apparently wanted a known director like Ford to helm the picture and not a first time one like Duke Wayne. He wanted to direct, produce and play the shorter guest star role of General Houston. Finally a deal was made with United Artists releasing the film for Wayne's Batjac Productions. Along with his producing and directing duties, he was to star as Davy Crockett.

Although *The Alamo* was Wayne's initial entry as a director, he was no novice producer, having produced his first film in 1947 (the Republic Western *Angel and the Badman,* with his *Alamo* scenarist and associate producer James Edward Grant directing). In 1952, Wayne formed a production company with producer Robert Fellows. Their two most popular pictures were the 1953 Western *Hondo* (with a script by Grant) and the 1954 drama *The High and the Mighty* (director, William Wellman). This last film marked the close of Wayne and Fellows' partnership, and Batjac was then created. The 1955 drama *Blood Alley* was this new outfit's first venture, with Wellman once again directing.

Wayne's financial advisor Bo Roos made some bad investments for him and so the money was not available for *The Alamo* before the United Artists deal. Generous financial support also came from other interests, including the McCulloughs and the Murchisons, a consortium of wealthy Texas businessmen. The initial estimate for the film's production was $7,500,000, but the final result was $12,000,000. To raise the capital to complete the picture, Wayne was forced to mortgage a home and Batjac.

Locations in Panama and Mexico had been considered for the film before

Wayne chose an area in Brackettville, Texas. Here, on "Happy" Shahan's ranch, a $1,500,000 replica of the Alamo was constructed. This Alamo Village, as it came to be called, was the center of film production for 83 days. It became a later tourist attraction; and the site was used again for the 1987 television movie, *The Alamo, Thirteen Days to Glory* (NBC; Burt Kennedy, director). For Wayne's film, 5,000 players were supposedly used. A few hundred crew and cast members stayed at the nearby abandoned military post known as Fort Clark.

The later television film was based on Lou Tinkle's book, *13 Days to Glory: The Siege of the Alamo*, while Wayne's version was derived from James Edward Grant's original screenplay. Certain aspects of historical value were overlooked in the 1960 film — including Travis and Bowie receiving joint command of the Alamo; Houston's ignored orders to blow it up; Bowie being a second cousin to Santa Anna; and Travis' drawing a line in the dirt with his saber and asking those who will fight by his side to cross over. For the '87 venture, James Arness was Bowie, Brian Keith was Crockett and Alec Baldwin was Travis. Raul Julia played the Mexican dictator Santa Anna and Lorne Greene had one scene as Sam Houston.

In Grant's scenario for the earlier film, Bowie learns of the recent death of his Mexican wife (she and their two children had actually died in 1832 from cholera). The Alamo defenders are also told of the attack on Fannin's men at Goliad (but the actual murder of Fannin's army of nearly 400 men, by part of Santa Anna's forces, took place after the Alamo's fall on March 27, 1836).

Despite any historical inaccuracies and excessive speechifying by Grant and Wayne, their *Alamo* is a far more moving depiction of the siege with splendid photography by William H. Clothier and second unit work by Cliff Lyons. Especially beautiful was Dimitri Tiomkin's music score. This stirring motion picture has many haunting images — "marriages" of sight and sound which make other versions of the story seem inadequate in comparison.

The actual Alamo was originally founded in 1718 as a mission called San Antonio de Valero. Abandoned by 1793, it became a symbol for freedom when the Texas Revolution began in 1835. Earlier, Stephen Austin had helped to bring colonists into Texas, and all supported the Mexican Constitution of 1824 (it was this flag which was flown by Travis during the Alamo siege). When General Antonio Lopez de Santa Anna became President of Mexico, changing his liberal policies into oppressive acts, revolution was ultimate. Twelve hundred Mexican soldiers under the command of Santa Anna's brother-in-law, General Martin Perfecto de Cos, were forced from the Alamo in December 1835 by 300 freedom fighters. One of the Texas leaders, Ben Milam, was among those killed in the revolt. The Alamo was then held by its gallant defenders until it fell to Santa Anna. One defender, Lewis Rose, escaped prior to the final assault, which lasted 90 minutes with all the other men being killed. Accounts vary as to the number of his men Santa Anna sacrificed; according to the Daughters of the Republic of Texas brochure available at the Alamo, almost 600 Mexicans lost their lives.

General Sam Houston, made Texas' Commander in Chief on March 4, 1836 (two days before the fall of the Alamo), brought together an army of nearly 800 American and Texan volunteers. On April 21, at San Jacinto, Texas, Houston's army attacked 1500 of Santa Anna's men with battle cries of "Remember Goliad! Remember the Alamo!" Six hundred thirty Mexican soldiers were killed in 18 minutes, and nine of Houston's men were slain. Santa Anna was captured, and after a brief imprisonment allowed Texas to become independent from Mexico. In October 1836, Houston was made President of the Republic of Texas.

A political force in the early life of Texas, Houston was its most famous leader. After Texas became a state on December 29, 1845, Houston was its senator from 1846 to 1859. In '59, he became Texas' governor until 1861 when he left office because the state seceded from the Union over the Civil War. Houston died of pneumonia at age 70 in 1863.

Although *The Alamo* only gives Houston two brief passages, they are among the film's most unforgettable. With great fortitude, Richard Boone conveys the charisma that made Houston the strong leader of the Texas Revolution. By 1960 Boone was starring as Paladin on NBC's *Have Gun, Will Travel* (the third most popular program on television from October 1958 to April 1961).

Like Houston, William Barret Travis had a sharp political awareness. He was a lawyer in Alabama when he was only 19. He became a leader early in the Texas Revolution by commanding a group of 40 volunteers and capturing the Mexican garrison at Anahuac. He died at the Alamo at age 26.

Laurence Harvey shared with Travis a flair for the dramatic. Unfortunately, Travis' famous message — "To the People of Texas and All Americans in the World" — eloquently asking for help at the Alamo, was not included in the film. Part of it is spoken by the actor on the documentary footage included on the MGM/UA video of the film. (Harvey's reading was originally heard on the ABC-TV 1960's special *The Spirit of the Alamo*, hosted by John Wayne).

Perhaps because of his hard-working professionalism in British films of the 1950s, Harvey was recognized as a highly serious actor. He was rewarded with an Oscar nomination as Best Actor for the '59 British drama *Room at the Top* (Romulus Films; Jack Clayton, director). On location for *The Alamo*, Harvey displayed a humorous side to his nature which delighted cast and crew. Yet his unflinching professionalism was also seen during the filming when he bravely carried on after a cannon broke his foot. His performance as Travis was superb.

Another impassioned performance was given by Richard Widmark as Jim

Bowie. There was alleged friction between Wayne and Widmark during production, and some of it may have been due to the latter's feeling that he was miscast. On the contrary, Widmark's acting background in films during the '50s, including both military dramas and Westerns, made him an ideal choice for the rugged adventurer.

Widmark received an Oscar nomination as Best Supporting Actor for his first film, 1947's drama *Kiss of Death* (20th Century–Fox; Henry Hathaway, director). He then signed a seven-year contract with Fox, appearing in his first Western in '48, *Yellow Sky* (William Wellman, director). He rode with Gary Cooper in Fox's 1954 Western, *Garden of Evil* (again with director Hathaway). Universal's *Backlash* ('56) and MGM's *The Law and Jake Wade* ('58) were Westerns Widmark made for director John Sturges. Perhaps the actor's best Western during these years was 1956's Fox entry, *The Last Wagon* (Delmer Daves, director). His hard-bitten frontiersman in this film was reminiscent of the physical bearing and authority he brought to the role of Bowie.

Jim Bowie's claim to fame, aside from his death at age 40 in the Alamo (he fought from his bed, having been stricken with pneumonia), was the famous hunting knife named after him. In 1827, in the notorious "Sand Bar" incident (alluded to in the film) just outside Natchez, Mississippi, Bowie was seriously injured during a fight but managed to use his knife with deadly force against his assailants. Although Bowie did not have a slave at the Alamo (as depicted in the film with gentle strength by Jester Hairston), he actually had smuggled slaves earlier with infamous pirate Jean Lafitte.

Davy Crockett, like Bowie, was a figure whose legendary stature became part of American folklore. His marksmanship with the long rifle was as renowned as Bowie's prowess with the knife. Crockett's own zest at story-telling surely added fire to his early adventures in fighting bears and Indians. And his oratory skills helped get him elected as a Congressman between 1827 and 1835. He died at age 49 at the Alamo. Whether he was killed fighting or as one of six captives taken before Santa Anna and then executed is debated but doesn't make his sacrifice any less honorable. He was the Alamo's most famous defender.

Crockett's legend was wonderfully explored by Walt Disney in five television programs, alternating on his weekly ABC show between 1954 and '55. The programs became so popular that they were edited into two feature length films —1955's *Davy Crockett, King of the Wild Frontier* and 1956's *Davy Crockett and the River Pirates* (both were directed by Norman Foster). Fess Parker became an overnight star in the title role.

It surely seemed that no one could fill Parker's coonskin hat until John Wayne played Crockett. If there is a figure as tall in stature, perhaps even more than Davy himself, it is the beloved Duke. He no doubt was well aware of

Parker's fame as Davy, and let co-stars Widmark and Harvey take the acting honors. Wayne chose a generally low-keyed amiability in keeping with Parker's own persona. But as a spirited man of action, whether as an actor or director, Wayne played second fiddle to none.

Wayne's son Michael acted as his production assistant on *The Alamo* while son Patrick had the strong role of the dashing young Captain James Bonham. (Wayne's last son John Ethan played one of the brave defenders in the 1987 television epic.) Three-year-old daughter Aissa also had a prominent role in her father's film as Angelina "Lisa" Dickinson. Her parents in the film, Captain Dickinson and his wife, Sue, were portrayed by Ken Curtis and Joan O'Brien. (Particularly heartwarming is the child's birthday scene where they sing to her the sweet lullaby "Tennessee Babe.") Linda Cristal was a most attractive romantic interest for Wayne's Crockett. Teen singing idol Frankie Avalon was given a chance to shine as the Alamo's youngest soldier.

In history, Bonham was a close friend to Travis; they had been children together and grew up to practice law. Almeron Dickinson was Travis' artillery officer at the Alamo; his wife Susanna and 15-month-old daughter Angelina did survive Santa Anna's attack. (Although not shown in the film, there were other noncombatant survivors to tell the tragic tale.) Cristal's Flaca, Avalon's Smitty and Chill Wills' Beekeeper were among those in the film who were colorful but not historical characters.

For his boisterous Tennessean, Wills was nominated for an Oscar as Best Supporting Actor. He lost the award to *Spartacus'* Peter Ustinov. *The Alamo* received an additional six Academy Award nominations — Best Picture, Cinematography (Color; William H. Clothier), Editing (Stuart Gilmore), Scoring of a Dramatic or Comedy Picture (Dimitri Tiomkin), Song ("The Green Leaves of Summer"; music by Tiomkin, lyrics by Paul Francis Webster) and Sound. Only the last category was a winner for sound directors Gordon E. Sawyer and Fred Hynes. The song award went to Manos Hadjidakis for "Never on Sunday" from the movie of the same name; the scoring award went to Ernest Gold for *Exodus*. *Spartacus'* Russell Metty took the cinematography award. *The Apartment* won the Oscars for Editing and Best Picture.

That *The Alamo* did not do better at the Oscars was partially attributed to an overzealous publicity campaign by Duke Wayne and publicist Russell Birdwell; among other things, they reminded Academy voters of their patriotic duty to the courageous men who died that freedom might live. An embarrassing Oscar ad campaign by Chill Wills and press agent W.S. Wojciechowicz, signifying that the actor's hopes for the award were in the prayers of *The Alamo*'s cast and crew, also was considered harmful.

The film's initial domestic box office earnings of over $7,918,000 would have assured it as a financial success if not for its tremendous expenditure.

Wayne never made any money on his dream film. He made sure that all who had invested in the picture were compensated, and he was forced to sell back his share in *The Alamo* to United Artists to pay off the debts. With a later worldwide release, the studio would see a great profit earned.

In recent years MGM/UA Home Video and Michael Wayne restored the original director's cut. Among the reinstated sequences are Crockett's killing of Emil, Travis branding Bowie a traitor for wanting to take his men out, Lisa's birthday party (which includes a reprise of the song "Here's to the Ladies," sung earlier by Chill Wills and now by Frankie Avalon) and the death of the beloved Parson (Hank Worden).

Reviews

Commonweal: "Although the faults in John Wayne's picture are mainly in its excesses, it deserves respect for its assets: its authentic reproduction of the Alamo as it stood in 1836 and its lively recreation of the inspiring Alamo legend."

Variety: "Most gratifying is the absence of any corny strokes when the heroes perish. These are accomplished with great dignity and ample meaning through dramatic and directorial restraint."

I can kill the first man who so much as whispers a word about giving up. The very first man, so help me, I'll blow his head off.

YUL BRYNNER *as Chris, to the villagers*

The Magnificent Seven

1960

The magnificent seven on the march: (left to right) Charles Bronson, Brad Dexter, Horst Buchholz, Yul Brynner, Steve McQueen, Robert Vaughn, and James Coburn.

THE MAGNIFICENT SEVEN

A Mirisch-Alpha Picture. Released by United Artists, 1960. DeLuxe Color. Panavision. MGM/UA Home Video. 129 minutes.

Credits: John Sturges (Director and Producer); Walter Mirisch (Executive Producer); Lou Morheim (Associate Producer); Robert Relyea, Jaime Contreras (Assistant Directors); William Roberts (Screenplay); Charles Lang, Jr. (Photographer); Ferris Webster (Editor); Edward Fitzgerald (Art Director); Rafael Suarez (Set Decorator); Bert Henrikson (Wardrobe); Emile Lavigne (Makeup); Milt Rice (Special Effects); Elmer Bernstein (Music Score). Based on the Japanese film *Seven Samurai.*

Cast: Yul Brynner (Chris); Eli Wallach (Calvera); Steve McQueen (Vin); Horst Buchholz (Chico); Charles Bronson (O'Reilly); Robert Vaughn (Lee); Brad Dexter (Harry); James Coburn (Britt); Vladimir Sokoloff (Old Man); Rosenda Monteros (Petra); Jorge Martinez de Hoyos (Hilario); Whit Bissell (Chamlee); Val Avery (Henry); Bing Russell (Robert); Rico Alaniz (Sotero); Robert Wilke (Wallace).

Synopsis

A Mexican village is overrun by Calvera and his bandits. When one of the villagers resists, he is gunned down by the bandit leader. After the bandits have left, the villagers are at odds on what to do since these raids recur on a regular basis. An old man living just outside the village urges them to buy guns and fight the bandits. Three of the villagers journey to an American border town to buy the weapons.

In this distant town, a dead Indian is being kept from burial in Boot Hill by a prejudiced group of white men. A drifter, Chris, agrees to drive the hearse up to the cemetery; another drifter, Vin, decides to ride shotgun at his side although the two men are strangers to each other. Despite loud taunts and a gunshot from behind a window (which Vin answers with a blast from the shotgun), the pair reach Boot Hill with the hearse. Two armed men try to stop them, but Chris disarms both troublemakers with his own gun. The Indian is then buried.

The three Mexicans go to Chris for help in buying guns. Chris suggests hiring gunmen instead since it would be cheaper; when he realizes how poor and desperate the Mexican farmers are, he agrees to help and spreads the word that hired guns are needed.

When an impetuous young man, Chico, offers his services, Chris embarrasses him so as to discourage him from risking his life. An old friend, Harry, joins Chris, believing he must be looking for gold or other riches rather than just helping poor farmers. Not keen on being a grocery clerk in town, Vin elects to join Chris although the job only pays $20 a man.

Chris and Vin ride out to a small ranch where they recruit a man (recommended by Harry) named O'Reilly. At the town's railroad station, a cowboy, Britt, is forced into a fight with another cowboy and kills him with a knife. Although acquainted with Chris, Britt is not interested in hiring on.

Later, Chico is drunk and calls out Chris for a gunfight, but he ignores him and the young man soon passes out. Having changed his mind, Britt arrives to join Chris. A noted gunman, Lee, waits for Chris at the hotel and agrees to join up to pay off a debt in town.

When the six hired guns ride out with the villagers, they are followed by Chico. His perseverance impresses the others and he is allowed to join them on the trail.

They all ride into the Mexican village, finding many of the farmers hiding in fear. Chico rings the church bell and reminds the villagers that he and his comrades have come to help them. Shamed, the cowardly farmers reveal themselves.

When three of Calvera's men are spotted in a nearby arroyo, Chris sends Britt to bring at least one in alive. Lee and Chico accompany Britt. Chico is forced to kill one of the bandits and Britt another. Lee doesn't even draw his gun. When the last bandit is racing away on horseback in the far distance, Britt shoots him off his mount. Chico is impressed by the shot, but not Britt, who was aiming for the horse.

With the rifles taken from the three dead bandits, the seven gunmen begin training the villagers on how to use the weapons. The farmers deny that there are riches in the nearby mountains, but Harry thinks they are lying. Their only deception concerns the whereabouts of the village women; after Chico finds them hiding in fear of his comrades, they are brought back. The seven mean no harm to the women and share their food with them and the children. All prepare for Calvera's next attack.

When Calvera rides into the village with his horde of 40 bandits, he is met by Chris and the others. A fight breaks out, which the villagers join in, and the bandits are driven off. Only Lee had not taken part. Soon, several of Calvera's men begin sniping at the village. O'Reilly goes to the aid of three little boys, beckoning them to stay out of the line of fire. Chris brings word that it is safe after the snipers are stopped.

Eli Wallach (center, on horseback) confronts Yul Brynner in a Mexican village; James Coburn (far right) and other players look on.

Without telling his partners, Chico sneaks into Calvera's camp to learn the bandit's next move. Meanwhile, Lee admits to having lost his nerve to two villagers, who understand his fear. The three little boys have especially taken a liking to O'Reilly. One of the village women, Petra, has fallen in love with Chico.

Chico's report that Calvera is desperate for food and supplies from the village creates panic amongst the farmers. The seven then have misgivings about whether or not they really are wanted, although Chris is adamant about not quitting.

In an attempt to invade Calvera's campsite, the seven gunmen are surprised to find it deserted. An even bigger surprise confronts them upon their return to the village; a farmer, Sotero, has betrayed them and the seven are captured by the bandits.

Calvera doesn't kill them because he fears that their friends will try to avenge their deaths; he agrees to allow the seven to ride off but without any guns. Prior to leaving, Vin shares with Chris his wish to one day settle down to a ranch and give up gunfighting. When the little boys call their fathers cowards, O'Reilly reminds the children of the heavy responsibilities their parents carry.

In the hills outside the village, the seven are able to collect their discarded weapons. Except for Harry, all decide to ride back and confront Calvera.

Riding into the village, Vin shoots down a few bandits in quick succession, setting off the ensuing battle. He is wounded in the leg but even then shoots his assailant. After killing a few of the bandits himself, Chris appears trapped in a doorway; Harry suddenly returns and draws the gunfire away from his friend. Harry is shot and dies in Chris' arms, still dreaming of lost gold.

O'Reilly, firing from a rooftop, is wounded in the shoulder and rolls to the ground. Facing his fear, Lee shoots down three bandits to rescue several of the villagers. As he watches the farmers conquer their own fears and go after the other bandits, Lee is fatally struck down by a bandit's bullet. With Calvera bearing down on him, Chris shoots the bandit leader dead.

Chico's bravery and the courage of the farmers inspires Sotero to help. Testing his own fortitude Brett kills three bandits before getting fatally hit with a bullet. Once more O'Reilly comes to the aid of the three boys but this time he is mortally wounded. Before he dies, O'Reilly has them look around at their brave and noble fathers who have helped to defeat the bandits. Seeing the fallen form of Britt, Chris picks up his friend's knife as a remembrance of his sacrifice.

Afterwards, Chico decides to stay in the village with his Mexican lady for, as Chris had earlier discerned, his roots are those of a farmer. As both Chris and Vin look toward the graves of their four fallen comrades, they see the children putting flowers on O'Reilly's grave. With the blessings of the village upon them, Vin and Chris ride away together.

The year 1960 was a big one for Western films, with John Wayne's *The Alamo* being the biggest. Wayne's mentor, John Ford, had visited that film's location and, to appease Ford, Duke had allowed him a second unit team to shoot some footage — at least one scene (the deaths of Davy Crockett's Tennesseans, played by Chuck Roberson and Rudy Robbins) was used in the film. Ford, however, would make his own Western in '60, *Sergeant Rutledge*, for Warner Bros. Also that year, "B" Western star Audie Murphy gave perhaps his finest screen performance in the "A" Western *The Unforgiven* (United Artists; John Huston, director).

Both *Sergeant Rutledge* and *The Unforgiven* were remarkable examples of racial themes being bravely explored in Westerns (1950's *Broken Arrow*, with James Stewart's white man daring to marry Debra Paget's Indian woman, was the great breakthrough film in this respect). *Rutledge* told the story of a black soldier (Woody Strode in the title role) defended by a military lawyer (*The Searcher*'s Jeffrey Hunter) after a white woman is killed. *The Unforgiven* had Burt Lancaster fighting Indians, his white neighbors and his racist brother (Murphy) over the love for his Indian "sister" (Audrey Hepburn).

John Sturges had explored racism in his 1955 classic *Bad Day at Black Rock* (in which a hostile white community harbors a terrible secret about a Japanese resident), and again in 1959's riveting Western *Last Train from Gun Hill* (where a lawman tracks down the killer of his Indian wife). This latter film, incidentally, was made by much of the same Paramount team as on Sturges' earlier *Gunfight at the O.K. Corral*— included were star Kirk Douglas, producer Hal Wallis and photographer Charles Lang, Jr.

An issue of racism opened what may very well be Sturges' best Western, *The Magnificent Seven*, when the gunmen played by Yul Brynner and Steve McQueen boldly confront the bigoted white element to allow the dead Indian to be properly buried. The film was based on Japanese filmmaker Akira Kurosawa's dramatic masterpiece of 1954, *Seven Samurai*, in which seven warriors are hired by farmers to get rid of bandits terrorizing their village. Sturges' remake may not be a masterpiece, but it certainly is, like his *Gunfight*, one of the most exciting and enjoyable Westerns ever made.

In 1960, Sturges became a partner in producing films with the Mirisch Brothers (Walter, Harold and Marvin), and their initial entry was this Western remake. Sturges produced and directed; Walter Mirisch was its executive producer. The screen rights to Kurosawa's film were bought by Lou Morheim, who was affiliated with Yul Brynner's production outfit, Alciona. Upon Brynner's participation in the remake, Morheim functioned as associate producer. William Roberts wrote the screen adaptation from the original scenario (which Kurosawa co-wrote with Shinobu Hashimoto and Hideo Oguni). United Artists distributed the 1960 film in collaboration with the Mirisch Corporation and Sturges' Alpha Productions.

Akira Kurosawa was clearly affected by American Westerns for his *Seven Samurai*; he admitted to being a staunch admirer of John Ford's Western films in particular. Although *Seven Samurai* takes place in sixteenth-century Japan, it indeed is easy to see how the story adapted well for the nineteenth century West (and Mexico) of *The Magnificent Seven*. In both films, the farmers are in turmoil over the bandits (in Kurosawa's film, however, the bandits do not attack in the beginning, but ride on intending to assault the village again after the crops have ripened).

Kambei, the samurai leader (Takashi Shimura), is first shown by Kurosawa saving a child from a thief; Sturges introduces Brynner's Chris with the famous ride to Boot Hill. Both incidents attract the curiosity of the townsfolk and serve to bring the farmers to ask for help. Unlike the Sturges film, where the farmers have a little money to give, in the earlier story they can only pay with food. Kambei (a dignified counterpart to Chris) is able to likewise find six comrades but in a much longer sequence in town.

The first samurai to be recruited by Kambei is Gorobei (Yoshio Inaba); later, when he is the second of the warriors to die, he is a reminder of Robert Vaughn's Lee (except that there is no fear angle induced, nor is there with any of the samurai). Kambei's old friend Shichiroji (Daisuke Kato) is a reminder of Brad Dexter's Harry (but without the hunger for treasure); he stands with Kambei at the end, the same way as Vin. Heihachi (Minoru Chiaki) is actually recruited chopping firewood, as is Charles Bronson's O'Reilly.

Perhaps the two most similar characters are Kyuzo (Seiji Miyaguchi) and James Coburn's Britt; both fighting men share the same laconic pride and the need to prove their skills to themselves. Their introductory scenes are identical as each is in a contest against a hotheaded adversary (Kurosawa has the test done with poles, then swords; Sturges uses the equally unforgettable knife against gun).

Young Katsushiro (Ko Kimura) is the counterpart to Horst Buchholz's Chico. Last but not least, there is Kikuchiyo (Toshiro Mifune), son of a farmer; his bluster and drunken foolishness in the desire to be a samurai also are reminders of Chico. The winning humor of Shichiroji, Gorobei and Heihachi compares favorably to Steve McQueen's Vin.

Seven Samurai is generally regarded as a better film than *The Magnificent Seven* for its epic focus upon the same theme — that of bonding individual courage and honor with a group to form a cohesive force against supposedly insurmountable odds. But its very length (over three hours) overwhelms the viewer — an extremely long time is spent recruiting the seven samurai, building defenses and training the farmers in the village for the impending bandits' attack. Kurosawa also edited; his supreme achievements as a filmmaker here are the exhilarating action scenes and the feeling of spiritual camaraderie. Together with photographer Asakazu Nakai, Kurosawa pioneered having multiple cameras set up for each scene. This format allowed the opportunity to choose the very best angle photographed.

John Sturges' remake (with Ferris Webster editing and Charles Lang, Jr., photographing) actually had a major advantage over the Japanese film by simply being the shorter of the two and having a tighter pace. Only three rifles are used in *Seven Samurai*, with all four of its fallen warriors being killed by these weapons and not the swords, spears and arrows they used against the bandits; the gunplay in *The Magnificent Seven* resonates with a more clearly defined, sharper tension. Surpassed here, particularly with the depiction of the final deadly battle, is the choreographed precision of Sturges' own *Gunfight at the O.K. Corral*. While Kurosawa's film may depict the furious mayhem of close warfare more realistically, the last battle (in the rain), although awesome, is slightly confusing to follow.

Despite the terrific physical action (the viewer almost has the urge to cheer at the various heroics), what truly sets off both *The Magnificent Seven* and *Seven Samurai* are the crisp characterizations. In the Japanese film, Mifune is given substance when his impassioned warrior reveals his roots as a farmer — he deplores the action of the farmers when he discovers that they have killed past samurai, and at the same time decries the past atrocities committed by other samurai against the villagers. Sturges has Buchholz's fiery Chico share a (less shocking) revelation. He and his six comrades were betrayed because the villagers feared not only Eli Wallach's Calvera but also Chris, because they are both gunmen.

Also given credence are Kimura's Katsushiro and Miyaguchi's Kyuzo; especially memorable is the former's youthful admiration for the other's bravery in going after an enemy rifle. A similar scene in the Sturges film has Coburn's Britt making a difficult shot and hitting a bandit much to Chico's delight.

Brynner's Chris and Shimura's Kambei are the strong, respected leaders who other characters play off. The two men share compassion for the frightened farmers seeking help. They also share moments of anger despite their usually stolid demeanors. For Kambei, it is when he chases after a group of the farmers who want to give up; for Chris, it is when he chides the farmers for wanting to quit over their fear of the bandits.

Unlike the one-dimensional bandits with their horned helmeted leader in Kurosawa's film, Wallach's bandit leader is a "charming" killer. His Calvera identifies with Chris' gunman although it ultimately helps to bring about his death (the bandit does not comprehend that the gunfighter is noble enough to look beyond any self-serving interests and return to face his adversary after being allowed to leave the village).

Besides the bandit leader, the seven gunfighters are all given well-defined characterizations by Sturges. Inaba's Gorobei, Chiaki's Heihachi and Kato's Shichiroji are the only samurai in Kurosawa's story not given more scope other than being amiable, hardy characters. Sturges dotes a bit on different philosophies — on fear (Vaughn's Lee and the farmers); on bravery (Bronson's O'Reilly and the children); even on greed (Dexter's Harry). His gunmen are likewise richly rewarded (even in death) for their self-sacrifice. The reward, whether for samurai or gunfighters, is in standing together to help those in need against an injustice.

While Kurosawa shows children in his film, Sturges makes his children's affection for O'Reilly the most touching aspect of his own film. When the little boys bring flowers to O'Reilly's grave, it surely echoes the haunting vision in *Seven Samurai* when Kambei, Schichiroji and Katshushiro stand beneath the four burial mounds on the hill (with a sword in each mound).

In *The Magnificent Seven*, Steve McQueen was given third billing behind Brynner and Wallach. He did not yet have their acting credentials, but he rapidly became a major film star thanks in large part to this film and also to a pair of war dramas for Sturges (1959's *Never So Few* and 1963's *The Great Escape*). A cool, tough yet sensitive screen persona made him an international star. Even while he was electrifying audiences with his disarming smile and lightning speed with a gun as Vin, McQueen was well established as a television star portraying bounty hunter Josh Randall on the CBS Western series *Wanted: Dead or Alive* (which ran from September 1958 to September 1961).

Conniving and charming villainy were indeed part of Eli Wallach's screen persona after making his film debut in the 1956 drama, *Baby Doll* (Warner Bros.; Elia Kazan, director). Earlier, in 1951, he had earned a Tony Award for his stage role in Tennessee Williams' *The Rose Tattoo*. The befuddlement he displayed in the play as Alvaro and the dastardly villainy of his early screen roles helped him create his amusing but deadly Mexican badmen in both the Sturges film and in Sergio Leone's 1966 Western *The Good, the Bad and the Ugly*.

Richard Rodgers and Oscar Hammerstein II brought the musical *The King and I* to Broadway in 1951. Both the show and its star, Yul Brynner, became famous. His somewhat arrogant yet forceful masculinity, as well as an exotic earthiness (serving him so well later in films), were first given prominent display as the splendid King of Siam. The part (for which Brynner first shaved his head bald) earned him a 1952 Tony Award; the 20th Century–Fox film version in '56 (directed by Walter Lang) won him the Oscar for Best Actor. Also, in 1956 he portrayed the Pharaoh with authoritative power in Cecil B. DeMille's *The Ten Commandments*. By the time *The Magnificent Seven* came along, Brynner indisputably was a major film star.

Colorful action films followed for Brynner, and he returned as Chris in the '66 sequel *Return of the Seven* (Burt Kennedy, director). It was less successful than the 1960 film and had a more violent content, although the plot once more had the farmers being victimized by bandits. Robert Fuller took over the role of Vin and Julian Mateos played Chico. Incidentally, Brynner wore Chris' striking black outfit for his exciting role as the robot gunslinger in the 1973 science fiction film, *Westworld* (MGM; Michael Crichton, director).

Charles Bronson first worked with John Sturges on the 1951 MGM drama, *The People Against O'Hara*, and appeared in *Never So Few* and *The Great Escape*. He was with Burt Lancaster in 1954's *Apache* and *Vera Cruz*, but Bronson's first strong Western role was as the Indian chief (opposite Alan Ladd) in the same year's *Drum Beat* (Warner Bros.; Delmer Daves, director). As with McQueen, there was a tough yet sensitive side to his screen persona which Sturges remarkably brought out with O'Reilly and the P.O.W. in *The Great Escape*. A standout supporting player for many years, Bronson finally became an international star beginning with his mysterious gunman in the 1969 Italian Western *Once Upon a Time in the West* (director, Sergio Leone).

Having received an Oscar nomination in 1959 as Best Supporting Actor for the Warner Bros. drama *The Young Philadelphians* (director, Vincent Sherman), Robert Vaughn was creating his own cultured and articulate screen persona. As the refined Lee, he fully grasps his fear of being killed and finds the resolution to stand up and face it. The actor would go on to further acclaim as Napoleon Solo on NBC's spy series *The Man from U.N.C.L.E.* (1964–68).

Another strong actor, Brad Dexter is generally regarded as the least remembered of the seven gunfighters. This may be because he does not appear as proficient with any weapon as do the others (but his Harry is no less rewarding as he gives his life helping a comrade). Dexter was in Sturges' *Last Train from Gun Hill* the year before. During the making of 1965's war film *None But the Brave* (Warner Bros.; with Frank Sinatra directing), he saved Sinatra from drowning.

The 1959 Columbia Western *Ride Lonesome* (director, Budd Boetticher) marked James Coburn's debut in films. He played a likable outlaw chased by Randolph Scott (whom Coburn somewhat resembled with his own laconic and lean demeanor). In the Sturges Western Coburn began developing that cool confidence he exuded so well, and which would help to make him a star with the 1966 spy film *Our Man Flint* (20th Century–Fox; Daniel Mann, director).

Introduced to American films with *The Magnificent Seven* was the energetic Horst Buchholz. During the 1950s, he appeared in West German movies before first getting serious domestic attention in the 1959 British thriller *Tiger Bay* (Rank; J. Lee Thompson, director). After his success as Chico, Buchholz made a few more American films and then returned to the foreign market.

The concept of gunfighters banding together against evil was often exploited in motion pictures — Wyatt Earp and Doc Holliday were gunmen whose actions helped create that most legendary of gun battles. But many gunfighters were actually linked to banditry; two of the most notorious were brothers Frank and Jesse James. During the Civil War, they were Southern sympathizers with ties to William Clarke Quantrill's ruthless band of guerrillas.

After the war, Jesse and Frank continued their attacks and they may have been involved in the first American bank robbery, which took place in Liberty, Missouri, in 1866. Guns blazing, the James Brothers were part of other bank robberies and also the first train robbery. The citizenry sometimes even sided with the brothers (especially when officials accidentally crippled their mother and killed a stepbrother in 1875). The public had had enough of the stealing and killing by 1876 and stopped the outlaws and their gang from robbing the bank in Northfield, Missouri. Jesse and Frank fled to Tennessee.

The Magnificent Seven was filmed in early 1960 in Mexico. Upon its October 1960 release, it was given a modest reception domestically; however, like John Wayne's *The Alamo*, it proved lucrative with audiences worldwide. Its "magnificent" box office, hitting $11,000,000, played more than a little part in getting the sequel made in 1966. There were also two additional ventures from Mirisch Productions and United Artists —1969's *Guns of the Magnificent Seven* (Paul Wendkos, director; with George Kennedy as Chris) and 1972's *The Magnificent Seven Ride!* (George McCowan, director; with Lee Van Cleef playing Chris).

Guns was the most rewarding of the three sequels as it was comparable to the 1960 film with another strong story, this time centering on the seven's rescue of a Mexican revolutionary leader from a military prison. The last adventure, the weakest of all four films in characterization, had the always dynamic Van Cleef, hunting outlaws whose leader killed Van Cleef's wife. Apart from Vin and Chico in *Return of the Seven*, Chris' recruits were all new gunmen in the sequels.

Stylish action surely was plentiful in these Westerns, but none as grand as the first in reinforcing the myth of gunfighters committed nobly to a cause. Probably the single most memorable aspect of each film was Elmer Bernstein's rousing score. Originally composed for *The Magnificent Seven*, it was nominated for an Oscar.

Reviews

Time: "Technically, the film is up to big studio standards. Color, camera work, acting and direction (John Sturges) are competent. But the script (William Roberts) is what gives this Western its special dimensions of inwardness and dignity."

Saturday Review: "Despite the Orozco peasants, native potteries, and semitropical vegetation of the hill country near Cuernavaca, however, the film remains closer to the spirit of *Shane* and other big budgets cow country epics than to the exotica of its Japanese source."

Let's meet them head-on — halfway — just like always.

JOEL MCCREA *as Steve Judd, preparing with* RANDOLPH SCOTT *as Gil Westrum for their gunfight against the Hammonds*

Ride the High Country

1962

Left to right: Joel McCrea, Randolph Scott, Ron Starr, Mariette Hartley.

RIDE THE HIGH COUNTRY

A Metro-Goldwyn-Mayer Presentation, 1962. Metrocolor and CinemaScope. MGM/UA Home Video. 94 minutes.

Credits: Sam Peckinpah (Director); Richard E. Lyons (Producer); Hal Polaire (Assistant Director); N.B. Stone, Jr. (Screenplay); Lucien Ballard (Photographer); Frank Santillo (Editor); George W. Davis, Leroy Coleman (Art Directors); Henry Grace, Otto Siegel (Set Decorators); William Tuttle (Makeup); George Bassman (Music Score).

Cast: Randolph Scott (Gil Westrum); Joel McCrea (Steve Judd); Mariette Hartley (Elsa Knudsen); Ron Starr (Heck Longtree); R.G. Armstrong (Joshua Knudsen); Edgar Buchanan (Judge Tolliver); James Drury (Billy Hammond); L.Q. Jones (Sylvus Hammond); John Anderson (Elder Hammond); John Davis Chandler (Jimmy Hammond); Warren Oates (Henry Hammond); Jenie Jackson (Kate); Percy Helton (Luther Samson); Byron Foulger (Abner); Carmen Phillips (Saloon Girl).

Synopsis

During a carnival, a man on horseback rides into the town of Hornitos. Seeing people lined along the street waving to him, the rider, Steve Judd, thinks they are greeting him as he once was a noted lawman. But a policeman shouts at him to get out of the street, and Steve then realizes the crowd is doing the same. Suddenly a group of riders come racing up the street; the leader, Heck Longtree, is on a camel. Winning the sham, Heck, a wild-and-woolly young man, gets into a fistfight with a bettor trying to welsh out of the contest. A friend of Steve's, Gil Westrum, is also working a carnival sham at one of its stands as a marksman known as the Oregon Kid (he never misses using buckshot). Steve and Gil had worked together as lawmen in the past, helping to tame the West, but have not seen each other for years. Steve informs Gil that he plans on working for the local bank but needs help to carry the gold bullion safely down from one of the mining camps. After Steve leaves Gil, Heck comes along; it's apparent that they are acquainted and share a shady interest in the gold.

At the bank, Steve is forced to argue his worth to Mr. Samson and his son Abner, who run the institution, before he can sign the contract. Abner notices Steve's frayed shirt cuffs, and the latter hides the fact that he wears eyeglasses by reading the contract in the bathroom.

Later that evening, at a restaurant, Gil and Heck confront Steve about the job, saying they work together. Steve is less than thrilled by the young man's gall. When Heck shows his gameness against a bunch of rowdies from the earlier race, however, Steve is impressed.

The next morning, Steve, Gil and Heck head out for the mine in the High Sierras country. On the trail, the three men ride onto Joshua Knudsen's farm. A religious fanatic, Joshua is a widower with a lovely grown daughter, Elsa, with whom he is terribly harsh and overprotective. Given permission to stay the night in the barn, Steve, Gil and Heck first share a rather tense supper with Joshua and Elsa, mainly because of the farmer's Bible-quoting. After the meal, Gil and Steve reflect on a lost love of the latter's, a lady who decided to marry a rancher because she thought a lawman's job was too dangerous. Meanwhile, Heck and Elsa take a shine to each other, yet she admits to being engaged to a miner, Billy Hammond. Her father scolds her for being with Heck; Joshua also dislikes Billy and slaps Elsa for talking back.

In the morning, Heck, Gil and Steve move on; later in the day, Steve bathes his aching feet in a stream. Heck seems to have little respect for the older man. Gil often has to remind Heck of Steve's fine character, but admits that he would try to stop his old friend if prevented from taking the gold.

Soon Elsa catches up to them, and Gil and Steve reluctantly agree to escort her to the mining camp of Coarse Gold, where they are headed anyway, so she can marry Billy. While the two older friends are sharing a laugh over a past memory, Heck tries to take advantage of Elsa. She protests, however, and Steve comes to her aid only to be knocked down by an unexpected fist in the face from Heck. Steve then knocks Heck flat with his own fist. Gil also hammers one home on Heck's jaw.

At Coarse Gold, while Steve and Gil begin collecting the gold from the miners, Heck takes Elsa to Billy. At first excited about seeing her betrothed, Elsa soon realizes that Billy and his brothers Sylvus, Elder, Jimmy and Henry are terribly crude and far wilder than Heck ever appeared to be. Billy is clearly the best of the Hammonds until he starts drinking heavily at the wedding.

Elsa is repulsed that the ceremony takes place in the local brothel. Afterwards, Billy is nasty to her and, when he momentarily knocks himself out falling off a chair, Sylvus and Henry try to force themselves on her. Elsa's cries immediately bring Heck and Steve to her rescue. When she does not want to stay with Billy, they take her away despite the protests of the Hammonds.

The following day, there is a miner's court to determine Elsa's fate since she is legally married. But Gil secretly forces Tolliver, the whiskey-soaked judge who presided over the civil ceremony, to lie that he is not licensed in California. Elsa is then able to leave the mining camp with Gil, Heck and Steve. The Hammonds waste no time in beating up Judge Tolliver.

On the trail back, Steve tells Gil about his own wild, younger days before becoming a lawman. Steve further states that as he got older, he was reduced to working as a bartender or bouncer to make ends meet. But because of the gold run, he now prides himself on getting back his self-respect. Gil questions whether this feeling is enough, having suggested that they deserve much more.

When Gil tells Heck that he plans to make a move for the gold, the younger man has second thoughts because he has gained respect for Steve. But Heck consents to help Gil when reminded that they made a deal.

Later that night, the two try to steal the gold, but Steve catches them at gunpoint. Steve tells Heck to drop his gun belt, but tries to force Gil's gun hand by slapping him. Even when Steve puts his own gun back in the holster, Gil refuses to draw and drops his own gun belt. Steve then binds their hands.

The Hammonds track them down, thinking about the gold too. Steve gives Heck a gun, taking the young man's word that he will return it. But Steve refuses Gil's help against the five brothers. There is a gun battle. After Heck kills both Jimmy and Sylvus, the three remaining Hammonds ride away.

Later on, Heck is in a position to get the drop on Steve but returns the gun. Steve cuts Gil's bonds to allow him to sleep easier. Gil escapes during the night; the next day, he finds Sylvus' body and takes his horse and gun.

Returning Elsa home that afternoon, Steve notices her father kneeling in prayer and it is suspected that something is wrong. Joshua is dead, shot in the face by the bushwhacking Hammonds. As these three brothers open fire, Heck and Steve are wounded and then pinned down in a ditch with Elsa. Gil rides to their rescue and is shot from the horse by the Hammonds. He is only stunned and runs to Steve's side. As Heck cannot walk on his own Gil and Steve convince the brothers to face the two of them out in the open.

Walking tall and proud together, the two old friends exchange gunfire with the Hammonds. Gil is shot in the shoulder, the brothers are killed and Steve is mortally wounded. Not wanting the young couple, who are now in love, to see him dying, Steve has Gil motion to them not to come over. Gil tells Steve that he will deliver the gold to the bank, just like he would have done. The two men bid each other farewell. Gil joins Elsa and Heck. Steve looks one last time at the distant mountains before he dies.

In 1961, John Ford made *Two Rode Together* for Columbia. Its tale of the search for white captives held by Indians was reminiscent of *The Searchers* (this time around with Richard Widmark and James Stewart). Its title could just as easily have fit for Joel McCrea and Randolph Scott in *Ride the High Country*.

Randolph Scott (top) and Joel McCrea.

Another 1961 Western, *The Misfits* (United Artists; John Huston, director), seemed to begin a trend, showing the Westerner as an anachronism in a developing civilized and even modern society.

So, by 1962, the Western format in more than one film focused on the passing of the Old West with its splendid rugged individualists. There was great irony in the fact that the very civilization the cowboys, gunfighters, lawmen and others helped to create out of a frontier wilderness sometimes had no place for them once their purpose was served. In 1962 three films emphasized the passing of that era with naturalness and a bittersweet sentiment — Paramount's *The Man Who Shot Liberty Valance* (with Ford as director), Universal-International's *Lonely Are the Brave* (director, David Miller) and, of course, *Ride the High Country*.

Ford's vision of the American West was always a personal interpretation so deeply felt and inspired. And when his own career was in its twilight he chose to reflect on the twilight of his West. In *The Man Who Shot Liberty Valance*, rancher Tom Doniphon (John Wayne) and gunfighter Liberty Valance (Lee Marvin) are but two sides of a coin, albeit good and bad, of the last vestiges of a fading frontier. It is a necessary change for progress but a tragic one, for Valance is killed and Doniphon becomes a wasted shell of the man he was once. Ranse Stoddard (James Stewart), a lawyer, survives because he embraces the change.

In Miller's contemporary West of *Lonely Are the Brave*, lone cowboy Jack Burns (Kirk Douglas) fights valiantly against a mechanized world he does not belong to. It is a modern frontiersman, the American trucker, who accidentally brings down the loner and his horse.

But MGM's *Ride the High Country* is the most elegiac of the three with its autumnal story of two old ex-lawmen, Gil Westrum and Steve Judd, who share one last ride together. Its tale is set between Ford's and Miller's at the turn of the century, and an automobile is fleetingly shown in the beginning trying to push Joel McCrea's Steve out of the way (it is a symbol that his kind is not needed). Randolph Scott's Gil is forced to parody their past legendary status in a sideshow (a symbol that this is what is only needed now). They had helped to tame many a Western town but civilization took away their dignity by stripping them of their usefulness.

Director Sam Peckinpah introduces these two characters with gentle humor and with a bit of frustration which is charmingly personalized throughout the film. He certainly made his most eloquent Western here. The true fondness Peckinpah had for his pair of protagonists would only allow the two actors to hand in their very best performances. What Peckinpah does with Gil and Steve that Ford doesn't do with Doniphon nor Miller with Burns is to allow them to retain their dignity in the end. By this standard alone, *Ride the High Country* may be the finest Western on the aging West.

In 1954, Walter Wanger, then head of Allied Artists, made Peckinpah an assistant casting director on a prison film, *Riot in Cell Block II* (director, Don Siegel). Peckinpah became a dialogue director with Siegel on other films, and with director Jacques Tourneur on two 1955 Westerns starring Joel McCrea —

Wichita and United Artists' *Stranger on Horseback*. In the 1955–1956 television season, he wrote a dozen scripts for *Gunsmoke*, of which ten (adaptations of the radio series) were produced. One of the two original stories was produced on *Dick Powell's Zane Grey Theater* (CBS, 1958), and it became the pilot show for ABC's *The Rifleman*. Peckinpah directed for the first time (also in '58) for another ABC Western series, *Broken Arrow*. He wrote and directed other Western programs as well, including NBC's *The Westerner*, which, like *The Rifleman*, was his creation. Only 13 episodes of *The Westerner* were produced in 1959–1960, but its star Brian Keith, contracted to the Western film, *The Deadly Companions*, helped Peckinpah to get his first feature as a director with this 1961 Pathe-America production. *Ride the High Country* was his second film as a director.

The film's producer, Richard E. Lyons, first came across N.B. Stone, Jr.'s original screenplay through writer William Roberts (famed for his *The Magnificent Seven* screenplay). But the first draft, entitled *Guns in the Afternoon*, was so bad that Roberts did an uncredited rewrite — apparently the substance of Stone's story was flawed, not having the natural quality sought. Peckinpah was Lyon's first and only choice as director, having liked what he did with the naturalistic feel on *The Westerner* series. Once hired, he commenced, with the producer's approval, to do further rewriting on the screenplay.

Like Roberts, Peckinpah was an uncredited writer on the film but, unlike him, had tried to get a writing credit. According to the Writers Guild, Peckinpah did not contribute at least half of the story to merit a credit; ironically, both Lyons and Joel McCrea said their director did rewrite more than 50 percent of the dialogue alone. Neither McCrea nor Randolph Scott had been particularly enthused with the original story until Peckinpah added improvements.

Between the two ex-lawmen, there were added ingratiating touches. Gil wears red long johns to symbolize his devilish intentions (he wants to steal the gold), and Steve wears white long johns to symbolize his godlike nature (he is honor-bound to bring the gold back). Both men keep their cowboy hats on much of the time, even in their underwear, to reflect on their images as saddlesore and enduring Westerners.

Peckinpah really had a field day with the five Hammonds. Their raunchy brand of humor is played out so broadly as to make their wild antics all the more frightening. Yet the three remaining brothers are given the semblance of family honor when they face off against Steve and Gil.

The single greatest change that Peckinpah made in the story was the ending. Gil was originally to die, as an act of redemption, after coming to his friend's side. Against the traditional Hollywood standard of the good guy surviving, it is Steve who dies instead; having already earned his self-respect, he is given his wish to enter his "house justified." The themes of loyalty and self-respect, tested under adversity, were prevalent ones in much of Peckinpah's work.

Randolph Scott and Joel McCrea, actual friends, were already signed for the picture when Peckinpah came on the scene. McCrea was also a friend of Richard Lyons and allowed the producer to talk him out of a short retirement to play Gil Westrum. Then writer Burt Kennedy, who had worked with Scott previously, was asked to get the actor to play Steve Judd and he accepted. McCrea had a change of heart and wanted to play the good guy, and Scott admitted to wanting to play the bad/good guy. They switched roles, with Scott winning a coin toss for first billing.

Gary Cooper was supposedly considered for the part of Steve before his death of cancer in the spring of 1961. *Ride the High Country* was filmed that autumn. Having continued to make Westerns after *High Noon*, Coop was in, among others, the even more profitable *Vera Cruz* in 1954 (with Burt Lancaster). Other Cooper Westerns of the 1950s included United Artists' *Man of the West* (1958), and Warner Bros.' *The Hanging Tree* ('59).

Like Cooper, McCrea and Scott had started out as extras in films. Scott, in a bit part, and McCrea, in a featured part, were in MGM's 1929 drama, *Dynamite* (Cecil B. DeMille, director). On *The Virginian* in '29, Scott was Cooper's dialogue coach. As Coop did before him in the 1920s, Scott appeared in a series of "B" Westerns which were based on the stories of Zane Grey (these were made between 1932 and 1935, and were directed by Henry Hathaway).

Scott got his first big Western in '36 (*The Last of the Mohicans*). Scott got his a year later (*Wells Fargo*). In the booming Western year of 1939, both actors were in two of the biggest—Joel in Paramount's *Union Pacific* (for DeMille) and Randolph in *Jesse James* (Tyrone Power had the title role).

Following the war, both McCrea and Scott devoted their careers to Westerns. McCrea starred in Paramount's remake of *The Virginian* in 1946 (Stuart Gilmore, director) and Scott made *Abilene Town* for United Artists (the first in a series of Westerns with director Edwin L. Marin). In '49, McCrea played his own Western badman in Warner Bros.' *Colorado Territory* (Raoul Walsh, director).

In the great Western decade of the 1950s, Joel made a film (MGM's *Stars in My Crown*) of which he was especially proud; it was his first of three pictures with director Jacques Tourneur. Scott and directors Andre de Toth and Budd Boetticher collaborated on two series of hard-hitting Westerns. The seven films with Boetticher, while considered "B" Westerns, were among the best of Scott's work — Warner Bros.' *Seven Men from Now* was the first in 1956, and Columbia's *Comanche Station* in '60 was the last. In the 1959–1960 television season, McCrea starred with his son Jody on NBC's Western series, *Wichita Town*.

In the vein of Gary Cooper and John Wayne, Joel McCrea and Randolph Scott were soft-spoken early on in their respective film careers. Growing older, they exhibited the same grittiness and toughness. Yet each had his own style.

Sam Peckinpah personally chose Mariette Hartley and Ron Starr for the roles of Elsa and Heck because he liked their fresh, "new" faces. Both gave exceptional performances as the young couple who discover what true caring and respect really are from the two pros, Scott and McCrea. Elsa at first is only interested in getting away from her oppressive father and marries hastily to do so; Heck is wild and cocky, a little like the Hammonds, until he squares off against both Steve and Gil (seeing the crudeness of the five brothers also opens his eyes).

Elsa's father Joshua was played by the solid R.G. Armstrong with tormented self-righteousness. While Joshua and Steve both share an interest in the Bible, the farmer is unbending and is actually a destructive influence; the ex-lawman, on the other hand, realizes the fragility in people and is thus fair-minded. Gil may have the more colorful sense of humor, but it is Steve who sets the example for his friends to emulate.

Even the Hammonds, whom Peckinpah also cast, are affected at the film's climax by the loyalty and code of honor of Steve and Gil. James Drury's charming Billy is clearly the most attractive physically and morally, of the brothers. In September 1962, just three months after the June opening of *Ride the High Country*, Drury began making a name for himself in a big way in the title role of NBC's Western series *The Virginian*.

Edgar Buchanan contributed his usual fine performance as the drunken judge (the actor had appeared in supporting roles in many Westerns over the years, including as one of the homesteaders in *Shane*). Both Buchanan and Armstrong's characters contrast specifically with Scott and McCrea's — the boozer and the zealot, like the Hammonds, represent the extremes of mankind, and there are only hints at the self-respect that the ex-lawmen are fortunate enough to maintain.

An area of the California High Sierras, at Mammoth Lake in Inyo National Park, was one of the locations chosen for the production. Photographer Lucien Ballard managed some very beautiful shots of the lake, forest and mountains before MGM changed locations (the new site was Griffith Park's Bronson Canyon in Hollywood). Additional filming sites included the studio back lot and the 20th Century–Fox Ranch.

In the actual Sierra Nevada foothills of California, in the Sacramento Valley, John Sutter built a sawmill in 1847. An employee, James Marshall, found gold there in 1848 and word of the strike became a world event. In 1849, the first fortune hunters called the Forty-Niners, arrived by steamship to look for the precious metal in the valley. Before the year was ended, tens of thousands of people came overland or by sea. In time, the gold was played out but several million dollars worth had passed through San Francisco banks. Miners, like those in the film, would move into the High Sierras in the years ahead.

Ride the High Country was made for the modest sum of $813,000. At the time, there were creative differences between top MGM executives Sol Siegel and Joseph Vogel. While Siegel supported Peckinpah on the film, Vogel had little faith in him. Hence the Western was placed on the bottom half of a double feature either with the studio's adventure film *The Tartars* or its comedy *Boys' Night Out*. For this reason, the film was not profitable domestically, although the critical praise was overwhelming.

Abroad, the Western proved to be a hit. In England, it was called by its original title, *Guns in the Afternoon*. By 1963, the film had won several foreign awards, including the Grand Prix at the Belgium International Film Festival and the Silver Goddess from the Mexican Film Festival. However, like *The Searchers*, it did not receive a single Academy Award nomination.

While the movie sometimes had a conventional feel about it, most comparable to the Westerns then being produced for television, its lyricism was exemplary. There was irony in the fact that John Ford was closing his career with his last statements on the passing of the West, while Sam Peckinpah was opening his film career with a similar perspective. Sol Siegel paid Peckinpah a compliment by expressing that he must have thought he was Ford after making the picture.

Randolph Scott retired from films after this one. The excitement created by the scene in which he and Joel McCrea stand together at the end in a blazing gunfight, with the autumn colors and mystic mountains behind them, is a testament not only to the Old West but to these wonderful actors. George Bassman's music score, Ballard's photography and Peckinpah's direction, particularly at this moment, conveys the nostalgic pleasure of their screen personas.

McCrea's death, as he gently lies down as if going to sleep, is one of the most poignant moments in films. Perhaps the best tribute to *Ride the High Country* came from Peckinpah's own sister, Fern Lea, who cried after seeing the film — McCrea's character reminded her of their father, who died the year before it was made.

Reviews

Time: "In the unhurried tempo of their speech, their ease of bearing, the firm-lipped gravity of their faces, actors McCrea and Scott give the action strength and substance."

Newsweek: "Within the standard cowboy framework, director Sam Peckinpah and screenwriter N.B. Stone, Jr., have created a Western that can be believed. *Ride the High Country* is pure gold."

Out of the hard simplicity of their lives, out of their vitality, their hopes and their sorrows, grew legends of courage and pride to inspire their children and their children's children.

SPENCER TRACY *as Narrator,*
on those helping to win the West

How the West Was Won

1962

Cavalrymen use a locomotive as a fortress in an attempt to deflect a buffalo stampede.

HOW THE WEST
WAS WON

A Metro-Goldwyn-Mayer and Cinerama Presentation, 1962.
Metrocolor. MGM/UA Home Video. 165 minutes.

Credits: John Ford (Director, "The Civil War"), George Marshall (Director, "The Railroad"), Henry Hathaway (Director, "The Rivers," "The Plains," "The Outlaws"); Bernard Smith (Producer); George Marshall, Jr., William McGarry, Robert Saunders, William Shanks, Wingate Smith (Assistant Directors); James R. Webb (Screenplay); William H. Daniels, Milton Krasner, Charles Lang, Jr., Joseph LaShelle (Photographers); Harold E. Wellman (Second Unit Photographer); Harold F. Kress (Editor); George W. Davis, William Ferrari, Addison Hehr (Art Directors); Henry Grace, Don Greenwood, Jr., Jack Mills (Set Decorators); Walter Plunkett (Costumes); William Tuttle (Makeup); A. Arnold Gillespie, Robert R. Hoag (Special Visual Effects); Alfred Newman, Ken Darby (Music). Songs: "Home in the Meadow" (lyrics by Sammy Cahn); "Raise a Ruckus," "Wait for the Hoedown," "What Was Your Name in the States" (lyrics by Johnny Mercer). Folk singing by Dave Guard and the Whiskeyhill Singers. Suggested by the Series in *Life* magazine.

Cast: Spencer Tracy (Narrator); Carroll Baker (Eve Prescott); Lee J. Cobb (Lou Ramsey); Henry Fonda (Jethro Stuart); Carolyn Jones (Julie Rawlings); Karl Malden (Zebulon Prescott); Gregory Peck (Cleve Van Valen); George Peppard (Zeb Rawlings); Robert Preston (Roger Morgan); Debbie Reynolds (Lilith Prescott); James Stewart (Linus Rawlings); Eli Wallach (Charlie Gant); John Wayne (Gen. William T. Sherman); Richard Widmark (Mike King); Brigid Bazlen (Dora Hawkins); Walter Brennan (Col. Hawkins); David Brian (Attorney); Andy Devine (Cpl. Peterson); Raymond Massey (Abraham Lincoln); Agnes Moorehead (Rebecca Prescott); Henry [Harry] Morgan (Gen. Ulysses S. Grant); Thelma Ritter (Agatha Clegg); Mickey Shaughnessy (Deputy Marshal); Russ Tamblyn (Rebel Soldier); Rodolfo Acosta (Desperado); Mark Allen (Colin Harvey); Willis Bouchey (Surgeon); Paul Bryar (Auctioneer's Assistant); Kim Charney (Sam Prescott); Ken Curtis (Union Corporal); Christopher Dark (Poker Player); Craig Duncan (James Marshall); Jay C. Flippen (Huggins); Barry Harvey (Angus Harvey); Jerry Holmes (Railroad Clerk); Claude Johnson (Jeremiah Rawlings); Jack Lambert (Gant Henchman); John Larch (Grimes); Stanley Livingston (Prescott); Edward J. McKinley (Auctioneer); Wendy Muldoon (Eve); Tudor Owen (Harvey); Jack Pennick (Cpl. Murphy); Jamie Ross (Brutus Harvey); Gene Roth (River Boat Poker Player); Bryan Russell (Zeke Prescott); Joseph Sawyer (Ship's Officer); Joey Scott

(Linus); Clinton Sundberg (Hylan Seabury); Karl Swenson (Train Conductor); Lee Van Cleef (Marty, River Pirate).

Synopsis

The Rivers

Generations ago, the only white people who had firsthand knowledge of the West were mountain men like Jim Bridger and Linus Rawlings. Leaving a friendly Indian camp, Linus begins traveling up river in a canoe filled with beaver pelts.

Whole families ventured westward when the Erie Canal was opened by DeWitt Clinton near Albany. The Prescott family — Zebulon, wife Rebecca and offspring Eve, Lilith, Sam and Zeke — are waiting for a barge to take them through the canal.

The Prescotts have sold their New York farm, intending to build a better one in Ohio. Urged on by her father, Lilith strikes up her accordion and begins singing "Home in the Meadow" for the Harvey family, who will accompany them on the journey.

After going through the canal, the two families build rafts to travel down the Ohio River. While they are camped along the shore of the river, Linus paddles in with his canoe. Welcomed, he and Eve take a liking to each other. Linus leaves the next morning, heading east to Pittsburgh to whoop it up.

Up river, Linus stops at a place selling whiskey, run by a Colonel Hawkins. It is actually a den of river pirates. Linus is waylaid by Hawkins' daughter Dora and cut with a knife. He tumbles into a cave pit which brings him back out onto the river. Only slightly injured, Linus follows the pirates, who have stolen his canoe full of pelts and headed down river.

Hawkins and his motley bunch set up a store to lure the Prescotts and Harveys ashore, where they are all soon held at gunpoint. But Linus appears, having floated down the river on a large tree branch, and kills three of the pirates in quick succession. This diversion allows the two families to join in the fight. Zebulon throws Hawkins while Lilith knocks down Dora. Hawkins is able to shoot down one of Harvey's sons, but Linus smashes a chair against the old pirate's face. Sam Prescott is among the injured in the melee, which abruptly ends when Linus sets off a powder keg explosion.

After the defeat of the river pirates, Eve wishes Linus would stay with her. Yet he still intends to head eastward after mending his canoe, damaged by the pirates.

Traveling on their raft, the Prescotts encounter rapids when they

The Prescott family tries in vain to turn their raft away from the rapids. *At rear:* Karl Malden. *Center, left to right:* Carroll Baker, Debbie Reynolds, Agnes Moorehead. *Foreground:* Bryan Russell.

accidentally take the wrong fork on the river. Zebulon is able to warn the Harveys to pull ashore safely. But the Prescotts' own raft is swept away in the raging waters. Lilith falls into the river yet manages to reach shore. The rest of her family are trapped on the raft as it is swallowed up by the deluge of white water.

Still repairing his canoe, Linus hears of the tragic accident and goes to Eve's side. Discovering that both Rebecca and Zebulon were killed, Linus helps Lilith and Eve bury them. The mountain man, now fully realizing his love for Eve, decides to stay with her. They will build a farm where her folks are buried. Her brothers will stay with her for now, but Lilith, who dreams of a different life, decides not to stay. She looks with anticipation at an approaching steamboat.

The Plains

War with Mexico brought vast new territories into the United States. Among the acquisitions was California, where gold was discovered in 1848. Many places were affected by the quest for gold, including St. Louis.

Lilith Prescott is seen performing in a St. Louis music hall. While watching her song and dance show, gambler Cleve Van Valen loses a hundred dollar bet on the number of petticoats she is wearing. He overhears that a late acquaintance has willed to her a gold claim in California. When some unsavory characters insist Cleve pay back the money lost on the bet (which was a gambling stake from them), he mentions Lilith's claim as a possibility.

Wagon master Roger Morgan tells Lilith she can join his wagon train bound for California, but only if she persuades another single woman, Agatha Clegg, to let her travel with her. Turned away by Lilith, Cleve follows the wagon train on a mule. To keep him from getting into a fight with Morgan (who wants workers, not gamblers), Agatha convinces Lilith to let Cleve join them.

When her fellow travelers seem forlorn one evening, Lilith brightens things up with the song, "Raise a Ruckus." Prior to this, Cleve had confessed that he was in love with her, but Lilith realized his interest was in her property.

Morgan also proposes to Lilith, asking her to settle down with him on his cattle ranch, but she refuses. When he catches Cleve gambling in back of one of the wagons, Morgan pulls him out. Their fight is stopped when Indians suddenly attack the wagon train.

Suspecting that the Indians only want their horses, Morgan has the wagons race on. The men are urged to unfasten each team's lead horses in the process. Seeing those around him jumping out on their horses, Cleve follows suit while Agatha uses a bullwhip to save him from an Indian. When another wagon overturns, Cleve, having freed the lead horses, jumps from his team to help. He shoots down a charging Indian. Concerned for Cleve, Lilith loses her balance and falls off their wagon. Morgan, who has had his horse fall under him, jumps onto a passing wagon team and picks Lilith up.

Following the attack, the Indians ride away with many of the horses. There is no sign of Cleve, however, and Lilith is worried. But he comes riding into their camp exhausted and she realizes that she truly cares for him.

Together, they go to the gold claim but are disappointed. It proved to be a pocket only which Huggins, the man watching the claim, feels entitled to have.

Lilith is approached by Morgan, who proposes to her once more and admonishes Cleve for apparently leaving her. Lilith doesn't blame Cleve for wanting a rich wife because she had wanted a rich husband. Although Morgan has a successful ranch, Lilith refuses his proposal because this is not the life she seeks.

While singing "Home in the Meadow" on a steamboat, Lilith is heard by Cleve while he is in a card game. Giving up a winning hand, he proposes again to her and she accepts.

The Civil War

The presidency of Abraham Lincoln was two years away when the differences between the North and South began affecting the free West. Lincoln knew the South was committed to fight and would try to bring the Western lands into the fold.

Corporal Peterson of the local Union militia, arrives at the Rawlings farm in Ohio with a letter for Eve from Lilith. It states that Cleve has become successfully involved with the railroad; Linus and Eve's oldest son Zeb is invited to California to join in the enterprise. Linus has already gone off to fight with the Union in the Civil War. Zeb, believing his father is having the time of his life in this conflict, wishes to follow him into the army. Reluctantly, with great sadness, Eve lets her son go. Another son, Jeremiah, stays behind with her to help work the farm.

The bloodiest battle of the war occurred at Shiloh in 1862. Among the many casualties there is Captain Linus Rawlings. Unaware of his father's death, Zeb is a soldier in the same battle. A rebel soldier runs into Zeb and, both realizing there is no glory in being killed, they think about deserting together.

They find Union generals Grant and Sherman discussing the rigors of the conflict. Grant, feeling the heavy burden of responsibility, is prepared to resign as commander of the Yankee armies. Sharing the burden, Sherman is able to talk him out of quitting. When the rebel soldier tries then to shoot Grant, Zeb is forced to kill his new friend with a bayonet.

After the war, Zeb, returning home, learns from Jeremiah that their mother has died. Gravestones for both their parents lay side by side (although Linus' body isn't really there). Jeremiah asks Zeb to stay on the farm. Having inherited his father's wanderlust, and not having been mustered out of the army, Zeb decides to go further West.

The Railroad

When the North and South were still at war, the East and West were coming together with the Pony Express. But these riders, delivering mail between

Missouri and California, soon gave way to the telegraph lines for faster communication. Then came the Iron Horse.

The Union Pacific (extending westward over the plains) and the Central Pacific (moving eastward from Sacramento) are in a race to see which railroad company can lay down the most track before they meet. One Union Pacific railroad man, Mike King, is angry when buffalo hunter Jethro Stuart brings in two men killed by Indians, thus stopping the track layers.

Zeb Rawlings, now a U.S. Cavalry officer protecting the railroad from Indians, knows that they are threatening warfare because of the violation of their hunting grounds. King urges Zeb to negotiate a peace treaty. Zeb then asks Jethro, who had been friends with Linus, to help since he can speak the Indian dialect.

There is a treaty that no hunters or settlers will enter the hunting grounds. King had said that such people wouldn't come for many years, but it happens immediately because the railroad needs money to continue building.

Zeb then tries to stop the apparent conflict with the Indians; when they shoot at him, he can only warn the railroad camp of the attack. The Indians stampede a massive herd of buffalo against the Iron Horse, causing destruction and death in the camp.

Afterwards, Zeb rides away, having resigned from the army because of their broken promise to the Indians. He says goodbye to Jethro, who has returned to the mountains to escape the advent of civilization.

The Outlaws

The railroad brought major changes in the West. Cattle were driven over harsh terrain to meet the railway lines for the Eastern markets. Rivalry between cattlemen and homesteaders broke out, as did lawlessness. But the men who wore the stars and enforced the law stood firm. Western towns were becoming more civilized much like the now large city of San Francisco.

Upon the death of Cleve Van Valen in this California city, his wife Lilith is forced to auction off their property to pay off debts. Over the years, they had won and lost several fortunes together. Holding onto property in Arizona, Lilith decides to move there with her nephew Zeb, who is now a lawman.

At the railroad station, she is warmly greeted by Zeb and his family — wife Julie and their three young children, Prescott, Linus and Eve. Also at the station, Zeb sees that an outlaw nemesis, Charlie Gant, has gotten off the train.

In town, Zeb warns fellow marshal Lou Ramsey of Gant's return. Since Gant isn't wanted for anything at the time, Lou doesn't wish to be caught in a blood feud between him and Zeb (it was Zeb's bullet that killed Gant's out-law brother).

With news that the train will be transporting $100,000 in gold, Zeb predicts that Gant and his gang will try to rob it. Julie doesn't want Zeb to go after Gant (yet she isn't told that the desperado made a threat against their family). Lou eventually does side with Zeb and they are aboard the train in expectation of the robbery.

Gant and his gang attack the train after it busts through a barrier placed across the tracks. Able marksmen, Zeb and Lou are quick to shoot down the outlaws one after another. In the furious battle, Zeb is caught hanging from a flatcar, with its load of logs breaking away, but still manages to shoot Gant. A partial derailment takes place and the outlaw's body is thrown from the train.

Afterwards, Zeb and his family, including Lilith, begin their journey to her ranch. There they will start a new life together.

The Old West won by its hardy adventurers may be gone now, but from the hardships of its pioneers came progress. They dared to do something about their dreams and helped to create the West of today.

In 1952, Fred Waller's wide-screen technique Cinerama was introduced. The initial motion picture *This Is Cinerama* (from Cinerama Releasing Corp.) begat a series of travelogue films with the innovative process. Audiences were overwhelmed by the photographic wonders that started with the thrills of a roller coaster ride.

Cinerama consisted of filming with three separate camera lenses — one shooting center, the others to the left and right — and then projecting the images onto a huge curved screen. In 1962, CRC, in collaboration with Metro-Goldwyn-Mayer, presented the first films to actually tell a story using Cinerama. These movies were the charming fantasy *The Wonderful World of the Brothers Grimm* (directors, Henry Levin and George Pal) and the grand Western epic *How the West Was Won*.

The latter film was a financial success with a near $21,000,000 domestic gross. (The film cost some $15,000,000.) With its incredible all-star cast and action scenes, the film was meant to be the definitive Western. Overall, it may very well be.

While the Cinerama cameras certainly captured a dynamic realism, sometimes the distinct vertical lines joining the three images are glaringly noticeable (such an example is after the buffalo stampede when Richard Widmark and George Peppard confront each other). As with *The Alamo*, this Western faced a barrage of criticism relating to its epic size. Some reviewers complained that the movie did not allow its many performers to have more depth of characterization.

The action sequences that make up the five interrelated stories of the Western experience are among the greatest of all time. Yet each character interwoven into scenarist James R. Webb's mammoth story (undertaken by three directors and four cinematographers) is a memorable personality. Standouts are Peppard and Debbie Reynolds (each seen in three of the five episodes) as Zeb Rawlings and Lilith Van Valen (nee Prescott). Also having large roles were Gregory Peck as Cleve and Carroll Baker and James Stewart as Eve and Linus. The film's focus was on nearly 50 years of the West's expansion (1839 to 1889) as seen through the eyes of both the Prescott and Rawlings families.

John Ford directed the middle story *The Civil War*. While it is the shortest segment of the five, it translates the finality of war with stunning pathos. Although John Wayne, assuredly the prime figure in winning the West in many a film, is only seen in a cameo as General Sherman, his drawn appearance echoes the harsh reality in the aftermath of Shiloh. Incidentally, Duke had already portrayed the Yankee general (also briefly) in a 1960 episode of TV's *Wagon Train* called *The Colter Craven Story*, also directed by Ford. This popular Western series, seen then on NBC, starred their longtime friend, Ward Bond.

William Tuttle's makeup on *How the West Was Won* was generally effective (especially with Peppard's lawman and Stewart and Henry Fonda's mountain men). But as the older Eve, in the Civil War sequence, Miss Baker's makeup is not entirely persuasive (nor is Miss Reynolds' aging process in the very last episode, perhaps because both actresses were simply too young and attractive). Ford's talent at poignant characters and depicting the bond a mother has for her child are on display during the touching interchange between Eve and Zeb (her eldest son with Linus) when he goes off to war.

Like Ford, George Marshall was part of the era of silent pictures when his own career began. His first feature as a director was a Western—1916's *Love's Lariat* (for Universal; with Harry Carey as co-director). The humorous overtones in this film were the stepping stones leading to Marshall's winning direction for 1939's comedy Western, *Destry Rides Again* (also for Universal). He had a knack for combining humor with drama as this picture demonstrated. But he was also capable of making more straightforward Westerns like 1940's *When the Daltons Rode* (with Randolph Scott), and 1955's *Destry*, a less successful reworking of the '39 classic (with the earlier James Stewart title role now played by Audie Murphy).

There was no comedy in Marshall's segment *The Railroad* in *How the*

West Was Won. But there were subtle ironies. The first is when Widmark's Mike King is set on firing Fonda's Jethro Stuart, yet he is the only hunter who can bring in buffalo meat for the railroad crew. These ironies escalate, thus creating conflict between the railroad and the Indians which culminates in the most spectacular sequence in the film — the buffalo stampede.

A herd of 1,000 buffalo were actually stampeded for the film at the Custer State Park, located in South Dakota's Black Hills. This fabulous accomplishment was done under the guidance of the park superintendent, Les Price. While shots are seen above the thunderous herd, there is especially exciting footage beneath the beasts which fills the viewer with a sense of danger.

Henry Hathaway, too, started out in silent films (he was even a child actor), but he didn't start directing until the talkies came along. His first film in this capacity, 1932's *Heritage of the Desert*, began the "B" series of Paramount/Zane Grey Westerns starring Randolph Scott. Hathaway's first major assignment as a director was Paramount's 1935 adventure film *The Lives of a Bengal Lancer* with Gary Cooper. Other Westerns for the studio included the following year's *The Trail of the Lonesome Pine* (with Henry Fonda) and 41's *The Shepherd of the Hills* with John Wayne. One of his finest Westerns, prior to his extensive work on *How the West Was Won*, was 20th Century–Fox's *From Hell to Texas* (1958).

In many of his films, Hathaway seemed to have a penchant for humanizing his characters as the story progressed amidst a lot of action. This most certainly was true for his work on three episodes — *The Rivers, The Plains, The Outlaws* — in the blockbuster 1962 Western.

Stewart's Linus has his sights set on staying free and wild in *The Rivers* sequence, like the wilderness he loves, until Miss Baker's Eve makes him a more responsible and caring man. The same concept holds true for Peck's Cleve in *The Plains* episode.

Like Linus, Cleve is amiable, charming and brave, but initially there is a rascally streak in both men which ends with each blessed by the love of an equally delightful woman. Cleve's love for Miss Reynolds' Lilith, and Linus' love for Eve, is realized only after each man has temporarily left their side. Yet all four main characters wisely choose to gamble on their love, thus fostering the growth of the West.

By the time of *The Outlaws* segment, Peppard's Zeb has an abiding devotion to family with the frontier spirit. He is introduced in *The Civil War* sequence with boyish innocence. The horrors of battle mature him, yet he still maintains an idealism when he tries to help the Indians during *The Railroad* episode. Although dismayed at times by his struggles, Zeb is never disheartened. He has always shared his father's wanderlust, but with his maturity (and that of the West as well) he fully grasps his mother's familial love.

From the very beginning of the movie, this love is shared by Zebulon and Rebecca Prescott (Karl Malden and Agnes Moorehead), who sacrifice their lives so that their children might have better ones. The role of family love in the winning of the West is seen when Zeb risks his own life for his wife Julie (Carolyn Jones) and their children.

Nineteen fifty-eight's *The Big Country* (with Gregory Peck and Carroll Baker) had showcased the epic splendor of the Old West as well. The fight over water rights between two families, the Terrills and the Hannasseys, could have easily been a part of *How the West Was Won* for its sheer scope and stature. One of the earlier film's writers, James R. Webb, went on to put together the scenario for the '62 Western with even greater scope and stature. The result won Webb an Oscar for Story and Screenplay — Written Directly for the Screen.

Many of the writer's characters were entirely fictitious, including the Prescotts and the Rawlings, yet intermingled with real-life historical events (the Erie Canal, the California gold rush, the race of the railroads and so on). Spencer Tracy's superb narration bridged the film's five segments with actual facts; part of these transitional scenes were directed by an uncredited Richard Thorpe. Webb's story was derived from a seven-part series of factual articles in *Life* magazine (from April 6 to May 18, 1959) under the title *How the West Was Won*.

Part One, *Opening a Land of Destiny*, mentions, as does the film, the fur trappers who first spread the call of the West. Also included here, but not in the film, is mention of explorers Meriwether Lewis and William Clark, who in 1804 led the first American expedition out of St. Louis, Missouri, and overland to the Pacific Ocean. As with the trappers in the Western mountains, the explorers had to depend on friendly Indians and contend with dangerous ones for their survival.

In the second part of the magazine series, *West Relives a Lively Past*, is an extensive article by notable Western writer, A.B. Guthrie, Jr. (his novel, *The Big Sky*, became a Howard Hawks film in '52). The writer vividly relates the pride American people have for their Western heritage by reenacting past events with shows, festivals and so on (like the Lewis and Clark exploration). He mentions, among other things, the importance of films like *Shane* (which he wrote), and the vast popularity of television Westerns.

Wagons Head Westward is the title of Part Three, depicting Independence, Missouri (so does the film), as a starting point for wagon trains. Their most traveled path, according to the article, was the Oregon Trail, ending at the same place (the Columbia River) that Lewis and Clark had journeyed to.

In the fourth installment, *The Great Gold Rush Days*, a reference is made to the bloodiest encounter with Mexico in California (at San Pasqual).

Following the Mexican War, the 1848 discovery of gold at California's Sutter's Mill is recalled in both film and magazine. Unlike the movie, however, *Life* states that John Sutter's property was often abused by the Forty-Niners and that he ended up poor. There is even an actual diary excerpt written by one of the gold diggers, Alfred Doten.

Part Five of the series, *Cowboys, Indians in the Wild Days*, chronicles the Western era's most famous years — the 1860s to the 1880s. As in the film, mention is made of the long cattle drives and lawlessness following the Civil War. There is a tribute to the cowboy in the magazine, as well as articles on the first violent Sioux uprising and Custer's Last Stand. And there is a particularly extensive feature from *Life* on gunman Billy the Kid, derived from newspaper accounts of the day.

The Frontier's Fabulous Women, by Robert Wallace (a staff writer for *Life*), is the sixth installment. It mentions the brave pioneer women who ventured West with their loved ones, yet also covered are the women of dubious repute in the various towns and camps. The magazine even has a showcase of such prominent ladies as Jessie Benton Fremont, who helped her husband John Charles Fremont (an early explorer), become nominated by the then-new Republican Party as their first presidential candidate in 1856.

The concluding seventh part is entitled *Fulfillment for a Promised Land*. Like the film, it mentions the Pony Express, the courageous mail service cut short by telegraph lines. *Life* goes on to state that the service lasted but 18 months (between 1860–1861), and that William Cody was one of its young riders. Featured in both *Life* and the film is the race between the Union Pacific and Central Pacific Railroads. Their eventual meeting, the magazine relates, took place in 1869 at Promontory, Utah. This final installment even highlights 1903's *The Great Train Robbery,* the first Western story filmed.

A 1963 novel called *How the West Was Won* followed the film and was based on Webb's scenario. It was written by the most beloved of all Western writers, Louis L'Amour. Previously, he had seen some of his own original stories made into films, beginning with John Wayne's *Hondo*. In 1960, with *The Daybreakers*, L'Amour began his magnificent series of books on the adventures of another pioneer family, the Sacketts.

L'Amour's novelization of the Prescott and Rawlings families closely follows the events of the motion picture. Yet L'Amour elaborates on many things not seen in the film in regards to further characterization, action and historical perspective. Beginning with *The Rivers*, he gives more insight on the Erie Canal, whence the Prescotts commenced their travels westward. In the novel, Linus shares the expectant profit on his furs with Lilith so she can realize her own dreams.

In *The Plains* segment of the book, wagon master Roger Morgan (played by Robert Preston in the film) is actually fistfighting with Cleve just prior to the Indian attack. Furthermore, unlike the film, Cleve knocks him out and is then forced to take command and circle the wagons. Later in the novel there is a passage, where Cleve kills a bear.

Unlike the movie, there is mention in *The War* segment of the novel of two small children by Eve and Linus who have died. (The film does show two unexplained tombstones, however, in the family cemetery.) There is also a description of Linus' killing of a clubfoot bear in the book. L'Amour details vividly the death of Linus at Shiloh. In both accounts, Jeremiah (Claude Johnson in the film) is left with the farm.

The differences between film and novel in the fourth segment begin again with a title change from L'Amour — this time *The Iron Horse*. One of several railroad men killed by Indians in the book, and brought in by Jethro Stuart, is Sam Prescott (Kim Charney in the film's first episode). Also not clarified in the movie is that Julie is Jethro's daughter (and one of the conflicts of interest between Mike King and Zeb).

The *Outlaws* segment of L'Amour's novel reveals that little Zeke Prescott (played by Bryan Russell in *The Rivers*) has grown to become an outlaw calling himself Zeke Ralls. A deadly confrontation takes place between his gang, Jethro and yet another bear. Jethro is shot and Zeke is both mauled and shot, and they are among those who die.

The novel also gives a more detailed description of Zeb's feud with outlaw Charlie Gant (Eli Wallach in the film). Both accounts depict the friction over Gant between Zeb and Marshal Lou Ramsey (in the film he is played by Lee J. Cobb). Unlike the movie, Zeb is forced to knock Lou cold with a rifle barrel (there is an unexplained bandage on the marshal's forehead in the picture). L'Amour has Zeb and Gant's shootout take place off the train.

Spencer Tracy's stirring words, bringing the Western movement up to modern times, closes out the film. The novel's final scene, included in the movie, is of Lilith joining Zeb, Julie and their children (Stanley Livingston, Joey Scott and Wendy Muldoon in the film) on the journey to the ranch which will be the new home for all.

This particular sequence in the film showcased footage of Monument Valley. Other locations included Paducah, Kentucky (where the filming began in May of '61) and the Uncompahgre (Colorado) and Inyo (California/Nevada) National Forests.

Although seen in London in November 1962, *How the West Was Won* was not released domestically until March '63. It received eight Academy Award nominations. Besides being a winner for Webb's script, the film won Oscars for Film Editing (Harold F. Kress) and Sound (Franklin E. Milton). The other nominations were for Color Costume Design (Walter Plunkett), Color

Cinematography (William H. Daniels, Milton Krasner, Charles Lang, Jr., Joseph LaShelle), Color Art Direction-Set Decoration (George W. Davis, William Ferrari, Addison Hehr — Henry Grace, Don Greenwood, Jr., Jack Mills), Music Score — Substantially Original (Alfred Newman, Ken Darby), and Best Picture (Bernard Smith, producer). 20th Century–Fox's epic drama, *Cleopatra* won the Cinematography, Costume Design and Art Direction-Set Decoration Oscars. The comedy adventure *Tom Jones* took the honors for Best Picture and Music Score.

Newman and Darby's collaborative musical efforts, like those of Dimitri Tiomkin and Paul Francis Webster for *The Alamo*, made the music seem grand and inspirational. Most assuredly a standout in *How the West Was Won*, besides its resounding main theme, is the lovely song "Home in the Meadow" (lyrics by Sammy Cahn). Debbie Reynolds' Lilith first conveys the pioneer sentiment and spirit through this song with her family as they wait at the Erie Canal, and again a half century later when she completes the Western odyssey with a new family.

Reviews

Commonweal: "Audiences who like their movies big, spectacular, full of adventure and excitement, sound and fury, should find *How the West Was Won* right up their alley."

Variety: "The story is far and away at its best when the emphasis is on the action, but the more intimate moments of the plot come out surprisingly well on the big screen."

When you side with a man you stay with him,
and if you can't do that you're like some animal.

WILLIAM HOLDEN *as Pike Bishop, to his outlaw gang*

The Wild Bunch

1969

Ernest Borgnine (left) and William Holden.

THE WILD BUNCH

A Phil Feldman Production. A Warner Bros./Seven Arts Presentation, 1969. Technicolor. Panavision. Warner Home Video. 145 minutes.

Credits: Sam Peckinpah (Director); Phil Feldman (Producer); Roy N. Sickner (Associate Producer); Cliff Coleman, Fred Gammon (Assistant Directors); Buzz Henry (Second Unit Director); Walon Green, Sam Peckinpah (Screenplay); Lucien Ballard (Photographer); Louis Lombardo (Editor); Robert L. Wolfe (Associate Editor); Edward Carrere (Art Director); Gordon Dawson (Wardrobe); Al Greenway (Makeup); Bud Hulburd (Special Effects); Jerry Fielding (Music Score). Based on a story by Walon Green and Roy N. Sickner.

Cast: William Holden (Pike Bishop); Ernest Borgnine (Dutch Engstrom); Robert Ryan (Deke Thornton); Edmond O'Brien (Old Sykes); Warren Oates (Lyle Gorch); Jaime Sanchez (Angel); Ben Johnson (Tector Gorch); Emilio Fernandez (Mapache); Strother Martin (Coffer); L.Q. Jones (T.C.); Albert Dekker (Harrigan); Bo Hopkins (Crazy Lee); Dub Taylor (Mayor Wainscoat); Paul Harper (Ross); Jorge Russek (Lt. Zamorra); Alfonso Arau (Herrera); Chano Urueta (Don Jose); Rayford Barnes (Buck); Fernando Wagner (Mohr); Bill Hart (Jess); Steve Ferry (Sergeant McHale); Elsa Cardenas (Elsa); Sonia Amelia (Teresa); Aurora Clavel (Aurora).

Synopsis

Six men in American military uniforms ride by a group of children who are watching a swarm of red ants destroy some scorpions. Into the Texas border town of San Rafael (also called Starbuck) ride the six, who are joined by two more men, and all proceed to rob the railroad office.

A band of riflemen are hidden on a nearby rooftop in anticipation of the robbery, but the robbers are soon aware of the ambush. As a temperance parade marches up the street past the railroad office, one of the employees inside is thrown by the robbers into the street. This sets off a chain reaction of gunfire between both armed factions and many innocent bystanders are killed.

Bandit leader Pike Bishop and his men — Dutch Engstrom, Angel, Buck and the Gorch Brothers, Lyle and Tector — frantically shoot their way out of town. Pike had purposely left another, Crazy Lee, guarding hostages inside the railroad office. The mentally disturbed Lee is shot down by the riflemen, but not before he manages to kill three of them. Still another of the robbers is also killed. Pike is forced to shoot Buck to put him out of his misery after his face has been shot away.

Harrigan, head of the railroad, had set up the bloody attack on the robbers. The riflemen are bounty hunters, and among their number are the filthy T.C. and Coffer. Their reluctant leader is Deke Thornton, who is given 30 days by Harrigan to either get Pike and his bunch, or go back to Yuma Prison and serve time. Thornton had a chance to shoot Pike during the robbery, but hesitated.

The Wild Bunch escape into Mexico with the bounty hunters dogging their trail. They rendezvous with another of their bunch, Old Sykes, and the outlaws argue over how to split the stolen money. Pike and Dutch side with Angel because a shootout with the Gorch Brothers over the money seems imminent. But the coins turn out to be nothing more than metal washers. The men are angry by this finding, but a strained camaraderie allows them to laugh over it.

Later that night, when the bounty hunters bed down, Coffer asks Thornton what kind of a man Pike is. The best, Thornton answers, because he never gets caught. While talking with Dutch about making a last big robbery, Pike shares with Thornton the same memory — they were once outlaws together, but the authorities cornered them in a brothel where Thornton was wounded and sent to prison (and Bishop got away).

Crossing over some sand dunes the next day, the outlaws are having a rough time of it with their horses. Tector blames Sykes and would like to get rid of him, but Pike tells them all that they better stick together. When he falls off his horse, Pike is taunted by Tector. But the outlaw leader climbs back onto his mount and rides ahead, the weary dignity of his departing figure prompting the others to follow. Sykes gives credit to Pike for his talk to the men about staying a team. However, Pike is taken aback when he discovers that Crazy Lee was the old man's grandson.

The outlaws spend their second night in Angel's village. A revolution is taking place in 1913 Mexico; the villagers support the rebel leader, Pancho Villa. Angel is told by Don Jose, the head of the village, that his woman, Teresa, has run off with a general from the government named Mapache. The outlaws enjoy themselves immensely in the village, carousing and dancing with the women, and are treated with great warmth by all the people. When Pike and his men ride out in the morning, the entire village bids them a fond farewell in song.

At a place called Aqua Verde, the Wild Bunch get their first view of Mapache riding in an automobile. In a jealous rage, Angel shoots and kills Teresa for being with the general. Thinking Mapache was the target instead of the woman, the general's soldiers almost attack the entire group of out-laws.

With Thornton's bounty hunters still on their trail, the outlaws accept a $10,000 contract from Mapache and his German advisor, Mohr, to rob an American military train for weapons and ammunition. Dutch and Pike con-spire with Angel to let him give to his village cases of rifles and ammo after the robbery.

On the way to rob the train, Pike tells Dutch about a bad scar on his leg. He was shot there by the husband of a woman Pike loved. Her name was Aurora, and she was then killed by the returning husband.

Thornton and his men know of Pike's plan to steal the munitions and are aboard the train. Once Pike, Dutch, Lyle and Angel uncouple the engine and munitions section from the rest of the train, Thornton makes his move. In the ensuing chase by the bounty hunters, and fight with American soldiers aboard the train, Angel saves Dutch from falling beneath the wheels. Tector and Sykes are waiting down the track with a wagon and the munitions are transferred over.

Pike then reverses the engine, sending the hijacked section speeding past Thornton and into the cars stranded on the track. Thornton's gang are sent plunging off a bridge and into a river by a dynamite blast from the outlaws. After their getaway, the Wild Bunch celebrate by passing around a bottle of whiskey. They break out in laughter when Lyle is left with an empty bottle.

General Mapache is in the thick of battle against Villa's revolutionaries when he receives a telegram on the successful taking of the train. The bounty hunters survive the explosion, and Deke is ashamed of these men forced upon him. He wishes instead that he was with Pike.

Angel's people come for their guns and ammo. Having surprised the out-laws, the villagers could have easily taken the whole wagonload had they wanted. A large detachment of Mapache's soldiers try to take the munitions away from the outlaws so as not to pay the $10,000, but Pike threatens to blow everyone up with dynamite to prevent this from happening.

Still not trusting Mapache, the outlaws bring the munitions into Aqua Verde in shifts. Pike is first with four cases and collects his $2500 payoff; fol-lowing are the Gorch Brothers and finally Dutch and Angel. When the last of the munitions are brought to Mapache, he blames Angel for the missing cases and takes him prisoner. Dutch rides out, knowing he is outgunned.

When Dutch is back with his comrades, he wishes to go in after Angel together. While bringing in the pack horses, Sykes is wounded by Coffer and routed into the hills where he is found by a revolutionary. Pike offers to give Mapache half of his robbery take after seeing Angel being dragged behind the general's car. Mapache refuses to free him.

Another bunch of gunmen on the move. *Left to right:* Ben Johnson, Warren Oates, William Holden, Ernest Borgnine.

Later, Lyle and Tector squabble with a prostitute they shared over her payment. Pike, meanwhile, is with another woman and her baby who remind him of the family he might have had with Aurora. Dutch is waiting nearby and apparently concerned over Angel's plight. Much to Tector, Lyle and Dutch's approval, Pike decides to help their comrade.

Armed, the four men walk together to confront Mapache. The general stands their tortured comrade in front of them and slits his throat. Pike and Dutch fire at and kill Mapache.

There is a moment of silence as no one moves, and the outlaws smile at each other because they realize the next move belongs to them. Pike shoots down Mohr, and this begins an overwhelming gun battle between the four men and the many soldiers.

In the bloody carnage that follows, Lyle makes it to a machine gun and uses it against the soldiers. Tector is fighting beside his brother when both succumb to their many wounds. In desperation, Dutch uses a prostitute as a shield, as another shoots Pike in the back. Pike takes over the machine gun from the fallen Lyle, but he is finally killed when a boy rushes out and shoots him at point blank range. Dutch, fighting at Pike's side, calls out to him as he also dies. All around the outlaws are the bodies of slain soldiers.

Deke and the bounty hunters ride in after the battle, and Deke takes Pike's gun as a homage to his one-time comrade. As Coffer and T.C. strap the dead outlaws to horses and ride off, Deke decides to stay behind, feeling his debt to Harrigan is paid. When he hears the distant sounds of gunfire, Deke can only smile at the probable fate of the worthless bounty hunters.

Soon he is joined by Sykes, Don Jose and the revolutionaries. As they laugh together, Sykes confirms that the bounty hunters were killed by the revolutionaries. As Deke and Sykes ride off to join in the Mexican Revolution, past images of the Wild Bunch are seen laughing and riding away from Angel's village with the people singing to them once more.

In the seven-year period between Sam Peckinpah's *Ride the High Country* and *The Wild Bunch*, influential themes of Western films included those of parody and the closing frontier. Among the best of the parodies was 1965's *Cat Ballou* (Columbia; Elliot Silverstein, director), with an Academy Award-winning performance from Lee Marvin. Among the best films on the fading West was 1968's *Will Penny* (Paramount; Tom Gries, director), with an exceptional performance from Charlton Heston in the title role of a saddle tramp who has outlived his time.

Old stalwarts John Ford and Howard Hawks seemed to have outlived their time by the 1960s — their films were fewer, while younger directors like Peckinpah, Burt Kennedy and Andrew V. McLaglen were making their own marks on Westerns. Ford's last Western was 1964's *Cheyenne Autumn* (Warner Bros.; with Richard Widmark and Carroll Baker). Hawks tackled a remake of *Rio Bravo* in 1967 with *El Dorado* (Paramount; again with John Wayne).

Kennedy and McLaglen both made Westerns which parodied and dramatized the Old West; McLaglen helmed 1966's *The Rare Breed* and, in a more serious vein, the previous year's *Shenandoah* (both of these Universal films starred James Stewart). Kennedy's Westerns included the humorous *The Rounders* (1965), and one with a far more serious nature, *Welcome to Hard Times* (1967). These two MGM films starred Henry Fonda.

Audie Murphy continued to star in "B" Westerns in the '60s, although they were not as popular as they once were. (The actor also had a short-lived NBC-TV Western series, *Whispering Smith*, in 1961.) On television, *Gunsmoke*, *Bonanza* and *The Virginian* were popular throughout the decade. In '66, ABC premiered a short-lived series based on the film *Shane*, with David Carradine portraying the gunfighter. Just a year earlier, CBS introduced *The Wild Wild West*; its tongue-in-cheek format reflected both the action and parody then in Westerns (with more than a touch of spy-film influence as well).

The combination of broad humor and rugged action were even played out in Westerns starring John Wayne. Among the actor's films were 1963's *McLintock!* and 1967's *The War Wagon*. Another old stalwart, Henry Hathaway, directed the Duke in 1965's *The Sons of Katie Elder* and 1969's *True Grit* (for which Wayne won his Best Actor Oscar).

But the films which really made an impact in these years were the excessively violent "Spaghetti Westerns," so-called because they were lensed in Italy or Spain. The culmination of this breed of Western was its foremost director Sergio Leone's 1969 epic *Once Upon a Time in the West* (with Henry Fonda in a rare villainous role). Ironically, the year before, *Firecreek* (directed by Vincent McEveety, and co-starring Jimmy Stewart) offered Fonda his only other vicious Western role.

The influence of these latter films and those with the theme of the passing of the Old West culminated in the decade's most controversial Western, 1969's *The Wild Bunch*. Released by Warner Bros./Seven Arts, the movie created controversy because of its explicit violence; the overwhelming bloodletting had instant notoriety.

Since the violence in films has certainly increased since 1969, this Western does not seem all that terrible any more. In fact, the film's power is relayed by the violence; it allows the wanted men of the title a chance to die as comrades united. This power remains intact because each characterization — whether it be outlaw, bounty hunter, revolutionary, soldier or citizen — has to contend with brutality.

Although Peckinpah made a more eloquent statement in *Ride the High Country* on dying with dignity and about the West's passing, these same sentiments are evident in *The Wild Bunch*. The shattering violence makes it a more powerful experience.

Film offers had not poured in after the critically acclaimed *High Country* for Peckinpah, so he returned to television and worked on NBC's *Dick Powell Theater*. In 1965, he directed the epic Western *Major Dundee*; the film was, however, so mutilated by Columbia that there was friction between the studio and Peckinpah. Peckinpah (who co-wrote *Major* Dundee) also wrote screenplays for two other Westerns, *The Glory Guys* (1965) and *Villa Rides* (1968). Peckinpah was displeased with the latter film's interpretation of Villa (rewriting had been done by Robert Towne). Pancho Villa and the Mexican Revolution were carried over into Peckinpah's *The Wild Bunch*.

Kenneth Hyman was a Warner Bros./Seven Arts executive in 1967 when he hired Peckinpah to work on the scenario for a proposed adventure film, *The Diamond Story*. But Peckinpah interested Hyman in a different screenplay:

through Lee Marvin, he had gotten hold of an original outline called *The Wild Bunch*, written by Walon Green and Roy Sickner. Phil Feldman was then assigned to produce the Western, with Peckinpah not only directing but sharing a writing credit on the script with Green.

Peckinpah's contributions to the story included adding the children torturing the scorpions with red ants (an idea he got from Emilio Fernandez, who played Mapache). He also wrote the two main flashbacks (Deke's capture in the brothel and Pike being wounded by an irate husband). The first flashback depicted the past relationship between Pike and Deke, and the other showed a possible family life for Pike instead of just crime.

Feeling that the violent content emphasized a part of human existence, Peckinpah highlighted it to remind viewers of the horror of it, not to condone or glorify it. What he glorifies in the story is the ritual of a band of tragic men who have outlived their time and are "playing out their string together."

Like *Ride the High Country*, this Western is set in the first part of the 20th Century, and the Wild Bunch's last stand is reminiscent of Gil Westrum and Steve Judd's. *The Magnificent Seven* and 1966's *The Professionals* (Columbia; Richard Brooks, director) also come to mind as the men unite as a team. Pike, Dutch, Lyle and Tector's climactic walk is reminiscent of those films in which the Earps and Doc Holliday strode side by side to the O.K. Corral.

Lee Marvin was the first choice to play Pike Bishop, but he chose instead to accept a more prosperous deal to star in 1969's musical Western *Paint Your Wagon* (Paramount; Joshua Logan, director). Peckinpah knew William Holden would supply the needed toughness for the role; the character of Pike seemed like a reflection of the actor's own hard-living, world-weary figure.

After making a name for himself in 1939 with the boxing drama *Golden Boy*, Holden's first Westerns were both Columbia entries — *Arizona* (with Jean Arthur), and *Texas* (with Claire Trevor; both 1941). Another Western stalwart, Glenn Ford, co-starred in the latter film which was Holden's first playing a badman (a cattle rustler). Holden's performances in two Billy Wilder-directed Paramount dramas, *Sunset Blvd.* (1950) and *Stalag 17* (1953), earned him Oscar nominations for Best Actor (he won for the latter). He was also in the acclaimed *The Bridge on the River Kwai* in 1957. Holden more than held his own opposite John Wayne in 1959's *The Horse Soldiers* (for John Ford), and with Richard Widmark in 1966's *Alvarez Kelly* (for director Edward Dmytryk).

Bill Holden's hard-bitten, assertive performance in *The Wild Bunch*, recalling past screen portrayals of wearied cynicism and opportunism, is one of his most exciting. The film is full of unforgettable moments demonstrating the undaunted Western spirit; one of its best is after Holden berates his cronies and falls from his horse. With as much dignity as he can muster, he climbs right back in the saddle.

Robert Ryan's equally sturdy Deke Thornton reminds the viewer of the haunting melancholy which pervades the film. His frustration with the pitiful bounty hunters allows this actor a performance totally in sync with Peckinpah's feelings for the Wild Bunch. It is a wonderful gesture when Deke carries off Pike's gun in the end as a homage to a bygone era.

Ryan was in another of the decade's most exciting Westerns, *The Professionals*. He was one of four soldiers of fortune (the others were Lee Marvin, Burt Lancaster and Woody Strode) on a rescue mission during the same Mexican Revolution depicted in *The Wild Bunch*. Both of these pictures displayed Ryan's skill at conveying a mixture of toughness and vulnerability. (Ernest Borgnine had this knack, too; both actors were also capable of giving totally villainous performances. They were among the town members who aggravated Spencer Tracy in director John Sturges' *Bad Day at Black Rock*.)

As Dutch Engstrom, Borgnine displayed his always formidable presence, and also the sensitivity which helped him win an Academy Award as Best Actor for his lonely butcher in 1955's finest drama, *Marty*. In *The Wild Bunch*, his concern is especially felt when, forced to leave Angel with Mapache, he rides off yet looks back at his comrade. Borgnine's loyalty, and Ryan's memories of Pike seem to make their characters perhaps the most heartfelt.

Edmond O'Brien's Old Sykes, the senior member of the Bunch, was an affectionate nod to Walter Huston's lively yet exasperating Howard in 1948's *The Treasure of the Sierra Madre*. Warren Oates, Ben Johnson, Strother Martin and L.Q. Jones had all acted for Peckinpah in earlier film and television projects, and their work here was among their most colorful.

Johnson and Oates have particularly large supporting roles as the cantankerous Gorch Brothers, but they are only a notch above Jones and Martin's fiendish bounty hunters. (The Bunch's final stand allows Tector and Lyle a chance for redemption.) The most unfamiliar face in the picture, Jaime Sanchez holds his own as the idealistic Angel. The Wild Bunch elevate themselves to folklore stature in their tragic gunfight at Aqua Verde against some 200 Mexican soldiers. Filming began in Mexico in March 1968, with the opening robbery at San Rafael shot at Parras. The final gun battle was shot in 11 days at the Hacienda Cienga del Carmen. The munitions train robbery was filmed at a site called La Goma.

The actual Mexican Revolution began during the presidency of Porfirio Diaz. The wealthy flourished while the poor languished under Diaz's regime. One wealthy landowner, Francisco I. Madero, spoke of revolution, and resistance groups were formed against the government. When Diaz was forced from office in 1911, Madero became president. Others opposed him, however, and, in 1913, a General Victoriano Huerta took control (and Madero was shot). One of the rebel chieftains who supported Huerta was Pancho Villa.

Many of Madero's followers united behind a state governor, Venustiano Carranza, who was attacked by Villa in 1914. But Carranza had an ally in one Alvaro Obregon, whose defeat of Villa helped the governor to become the new leader of Mexico by 1917. Prior to this, Villa began attacking Americans because U.S. President Woodrow Wilson sided with Carranza. Wilson sent troops, led by General John J. Pershing, against Villa, but they failed to capture the rebel. Ironically, the continual shifting of power had Obregon becoming the Mexican president in 1920, after leading a revolt in which Carranza was killed. Three years later, Villa was shot to death in an enemy ambush.

Following the 81 day shooting schedule on *The Wild Bunch*, another nine months were spent cutting the picture and making revisions. Peckin-pah brought back the actors (this time to Hollywood) to redub many of their lines for better dramatic effect, and the sound effects were completely redubbed. The newly-created Motion Picture Association of America wanted to rate the film "X" because of the violence, but an "R" rating ("Restricted — under 17 requires accompanying parent or adult guardian") was finally agreed on.

A 140-minute screening was released in the United States in June 1969. To allow theaters to squeeze in an extra daily showing, Warner Bros. had Phil Feldman recut and shorten the film. Among the cuts, much to Peckinpah's anger, were the two important flashbacks. While the domestic product was shown in Panavision, the foreign version was left uncut and shown in CinemaScope. In 1980 the studio was persuaded by Paul Seydor and Twyman Films to put back much of the excised material. The Warner Home Video version is the original director's cut.

The Wild Bunch made $5,300,000 upon its initial domestic release, and Warner Bros. claimed it was a financial failure. But it received a pair of Academy Award nominations — for Jerry Fielding's Original Score and for Story and Screenplay (Walon Green, Roy N. Sickner and Sam Peckinpah).

While there were viewers who found the violence in the story appalling, the combination of rapid-fire and slow-motion displays of spurting blood were not new to films. Even Warners used such methods to a lesser degree just two years earlier in *Bonnie and Clyde* (director, Arthur Penn). For better or worse, the final gun battle was transformed into one of the most fascinating experiences of direction, photography, editing and special effects. The story comes to an end as it began, with a bit of symbolism — the outlaws are the scorpions and the soldiers, even the citizens of Aqua Verde, are the overwhelming red ants.

The reputation of *The Wild Bunch* does not rest on this gunfight or any other violent action scenes. It is on the romanticism of this breed of men, who know that a bloody death is inevitable and make their last act one of selflessness.

Their lives are redeemed, their souls saved. The climactic reprise of the beautiful sequence in which the Bunch are serenaded in Angel's village shows us that their spirits do live on.

As originally written, these sequences were different — there was to be no pause after Mapache's killing for the Bunch to comprehend, with glee, that they had a chance for a noble demise, and only Angel was to have gone into the village. Sam Peckinpah filmed these sequences as he wished, making the Bunch into heroes. Therein rests the film's greatness.

Reviews

Time: "*The Wild Bunch* is Peckinpah's most complex inquiry into the metamorphosis of man into myth. Not incidentally, it is also a raucous, violent, powerful feat of American filmmaking."

Newsweek: "The men — William Holden, Ernest Borgnine, Robert Ryan, Edmond O'Brien, Warren Oates, Jaime Sanchez, Ben Johnson — have splendid faces and give excellent performances."

You never could shoot— not from the very beginning.

PAUL NEWMAN *as Butch Cassidy, to* ROBERT REDFORD
*as the Sundance Kid, during their last stand
against the Bolivian forces*

Butch Cassidy and the Sundance Kid

1969

Robert Redford (left) and Paul Newman.

BUTCH CASSIDY AND THE SUNDANCE KID

A George Roy Hill/Paul Monash (Campanile) Production. A Newman/Foreman Presentation. Released by 20th Century–Fox, 1969. Deluxe Color. Panavision. CBS/Fox Home Video. 110 minutes.

Credits: George Roy Hill (Director); John Foreman (Producer); Paul Monash (Executive Producer); Steven Bernhardt (Assistant Director); Michael Moore (Second Unit Director); William Goldman (Screenplay); Conrad Hall (Photographer); Harold E. Wellman (Second Unit Photographer); Lawrence Schiller (Special Still Photographer); John Neuhart (Graphic Montage); John C. Howard, Richard C. Meyer (Editors); Jack Martin Smith, Philip Jeffries (Art Directors); Walter M. Scott, Chester L. Bayhi (Set Decorators); Edith Head (Costumes); Dan Striepeke (Makeup); L.B. Abbott, Art Cruickshank (Special Effects); Burt Bacharach (Music Score). Song: "Raindrops Keep Fallin' on My Head" by Burt Bacharach and Hal David; sung by B.J. Thomas.

Cast: Paul Newman (Butch Cassidy); Robert Redford (The Sundance Kid); Katharine Ross (Etta Place); Strother Martin (Percy Garris); Jeff Corey (Sheriff Bledsoe); Henry Jones (Bike Salesman); George Furth (Woodcock); Cloris Leachman (Agnes); Ted Cassidy (Harvey Logan); Kenneth Mars (Marshal); Donnelly Rhodes (Macon); Jody Gilbert (Large Woman); Timothy Scott (News Carver); Don Keefer (Fireman); Charles Dierkop (Flat Nose Curry); Francisco Cordova (Bank Manager); Nelson Olmstead (Photographer); Paul Bryar, Sam Elliott (Card Players); Charles Akins (Bank Teller); Eric Sinclair (Tiffany's Salesman); Percy Helton (Sweet Face).

Synopsis

The Old West is fading fast in the early part of the twentieth century, but outlaws Butch Cassidy and the Sundance Kid hold onto the old ways. Butch, casing a frontier town's bank, is disappointed to see the stronger measures being taken against future robberies. Sundance is playing in a card game at Macon's Saloon, and he is accused of cheating. When Macon prepares to draw a gun against him, Butch intervenes in an attempt to stop any gunplay. The saloon owner refuses to listen until he learns Sundance's identity. When Macon shows curiosity over Sundance's expertise as a gunman, the outlaw, in a whirling motion, shoots the man's holster from his waist and sends his gun spiraling across the floor.

Returning to their Wyoming hideout, known as the Hole-in-the-Wall, Butch tells Sundance about his dream to go to Bolivia. The other gang members are waiting for them, and Butch's leadership is challenged by the towering Harvey Logan. The giant wants to rob a Union Pacific train instead of the bank Butch had in mind. Butch outwits Logan in a fight by kicking him in the groin, much to the amusement of the rest of the gang. Ironically, Butch decides to go along with Logan's plan to rob the train.

The Union Pacific Flyer is stopped by the Hole-in-the-Wall Gang. An employee, Woodcock, refuses to risk his job with his boss, E.H. Harriman, by allowing the outlaws access to the baggage car with the safe. The car is dynamited with Woodcock aboard; Butch shows concern for the man's injuries even as the safe is being robbed.

That night in town, the marshal makes a futile attempt to form a posse and go after the outlaws. Joyfully observing this from a neighboring brothel are Sundance and Butch, the latter especially amused when a bike salesman interrupts the marshal to peddle his merchandise to the crowd. Sundance, in a drunken stupor, goes looking for a woman.

In another part of town, schoolmarm Etta Place is startled to discover the Sundance Kid in her house. He forces her to begin undressing at gunpoint, but it is soon apparent that this is a game and the two are lovers. The next morning, Butch rides up to Etta's place on one of the salesman's bicycles and takes her for a fun-filled ride.

In a second robbery of the Union Pacific Flyer, the Hole-in-the-Wall Gang again come across a stubborn Woodcock. When Butch and Sundance pretend they are hurting a loud female passenger, Woodcock is tricked into opening the baggage car door. There is a much bigger safe this time around, and Butch, using too much dynamite, blows up the entire car, sending money flying everywhere. As the outlaws gather up their loot, they are surprised by the arrival of another train from which a posse of men on horseback swiftly exits. In the ensuing chase, two of the outlaws are killed, and the remaining four split off in pairs. As Sundance and Butch ride off together, they are upset that the whole posse rides after them.

Later that night, the pair of outlaws take refuge in the town brothel; they have an old man named Sweet Face convince the posse that they have left town. As Butch is all set to enjoy himself with a prostitute, the posse returns getting Sweet Face to confess. Once more the outlaws are on the move.

The posse is relentless in its pursuit, and the outlaws double up on one horse hoping that the riders will divide in different directions. Yet this ruse only works momentarily. In another town, Butch and Sundance desperately try to convince an old friend, Sheriff Bledsoe, that they want to join the army immediately in order to come under government protection from the posse.

Paul Newman (left) and Robert Redford.

Bledsoe points out this ruse is folly as well, that their outlaw days are over and they will die bloodily.

Again taking flight, the outlaws flee to the mountains and become even more desperate when the posse tracks them over rocks and up creeks. The pair speculate that two of the posse may be a noted tracker and a lawman. The posse eventually corners them on a cliff far above a raging river. Butch is for jumping, but Sundance says that he cannot swim. Butch laughs, saying the fall will probably kill them, and both men jump into the water. The swift current carries them to safety.

Exhausted, Butch and Sundance return to Etta's home. She informs them that the posse is made up of the most reliable men the railroad could find to kill the outlaws. To escape the posse, Etta agrees to go with them to Bolivia. The three then journey to that South American country after making a stopover in New York City.

The rural countryside of Bolivia is not what they expected. They take a stab at robbing a bank, but neither one speaks Spanish; Butch walks out of the building and leaves Sundance behind. Etta teaches them the language so that they can rob Bolivian banks, and she even assists them in the robberies. The thieves' techniques often prove very amusing.

When Sundance and Butch fear that one of the lawmen from the railroad posse has arrived in Bolivia, they decide to go straight. They are given jobs as payroll guards after the Kid shows his skill with a gun. Accompanying their employer, Percy Garris, down a trail to pick up the payroll at a bank, Butch and Sundance act like fools looking for thieves. Percy has to point out to them that they will not be possibly robbed until they have the money. Coming back, they are confronted by bandits and Percy is killed. Butch confesses that he has never shot anyone before, yet he and Sundance are forced to kill the bandits.

Butch and Sundance feel that they have no alternative but to return to stealing. Having promised herself that she would not see the two men die, and now knowing their days are numbered, Etta Place goes back to the States.

After another robbery, Sundance and Butch are confronted by the local police in a village. Both men are wounded many times before they are able to find a temporary refuge. As they speak wistfully of journeying to Australia, the Bolivian army arrives and surrounds the village. Butch and Sundance make a last gallant stand, fighting side by side, as the soldiers fire upon them mercilessly.

The Western parody dates back to silent pictures when top filmmakers like Douglas Fairbanks and Buster Keaton spoofed the Old West. Many a "B" film continued the legacy right into the sound era. One of the best was 1939's *Destry Rides Again*, a fine blend of comedy and drama. Jimmy Stewart's Destry, the deputy sheriff more taken with words than guns, helped to blaze the trail for dramatic stars to enhance their images in Western satires. Of course, there were also outright comedians like the Marx Brothers, who spoofed the genre in the following year's *Go West* (MGM; Edward Buzzell, director). By the 1960s, there were more serious stars romping through comedy-flavored Westerns than ever before.

Burt Lancaster was in a big one when he teamed with John Sturges on *The Hallelujah Trail* (1965; United Artists). But the apex year seemed to be 1969. Burt Kennedy directed two parodies for United Artists — *Young Billy Young* (with another great Western face, Robert Mitchum) and *Support Your Local Sheriff!* (with the equally sturdy James Garner, who mastered the art of the Western parody earlier on television in ABC's *Maverick* series). The most popular parody was *Butch Cassidy and the Sundance Kid.*

This delightfully entertaining movie soared into the 1970s as a blockbuster, making over $46,000,000 domestically. Its success was attributed to the remarkable mix of drama and comedy, and to the charismatic teaming of Paul Newman and Robert Redford in the title roles. Like *Bonnie and Clyde* and *The Wild Bunch*, the film had its roots in the rebellious 1960s in which a disgruntled younger generation made heroes out of social outcasts and even outlaws.

Butch and Sundance, while certainly unlawful, seem to break the rules of an equally self-serving society, one that is cold and mechanized. This is especially evident in the film's most suspenseful sequence, when the unseen railroad entrepreneur hires the enforcers to dispose of the outlaws, after they have dared infringe upon his wealth and power. These enforcers are always kept at a distance as a sinister, impersonal unit. On the other hand, the two outlaws are seen in frequent close-ups and, while they are anachronisms in a turn of the century West, they are not mercenaries like the Wild Bunch or the riders hunting the desperadoes in both Westerns. The Sundance Kid and Butch Cassidy reflect from the beginning a disarming amiability that is tremendously endearing. (Ironically, the Hole-in-the-Wall Gang was also known as the Wild Bunch.)

Director George Roy Hill was drawn so sympathetically to these two rogues that he didn't show their deaths (unlike Sam Peckinpah, whose slaughter of the Bunch was comparable to Vietnam War atrocities). Instead, as Newman's Cassidy and Redford's Kid are running together at the end with their guns blazing, they are immortalized in a freeze frame which then returns to the sepia tone opening of the film.

Like Peckinpah, Hill began a writing and directing career in television during the 1950s. Unlike Peckinpah, who worked on many Western properties, Hill's impact on the Western wasn't felt until his 1969 film. His work in television included the well-remembered *Kraft* drama about the Titanic, *A Night to Remember* (1956). For this program, Hill received a pair of Emmy nominations (for directing and co-writing). Hill was one of the foremost craftsmen in the era known as the "Golden Age of Television."

To do what he felt was more challenging work, Hill turned to the stage. Among the plays he directed was a Tennessee Williams drama, *Period of Adjustment*, in 1960. His first motion picture was MGM's 1962 version of this story. He helmed a handful of films up to *Butch Cassidy and the Sundance Kid*. This tale of two of the West's most colorful figures gave Hill the sort of creative control he had enjoyed earlier in his career.

Born in 1859, Sundance was actually seven years older than Butch, who refers to himself as the "over the hill" one in the film. Their real names (mentioned in the movie) were very different from their legendary handles — Sundance's was Harry Longabaugh while Butch's was Robert Leroy Parker. They teamed up in 1899 and their gang robbed banks and trains and even rustled cattle in Wyoming and Utah. Prior to Sundance, Butch's favorite cohort had been one Elzy Lay, who was caught and jailed. There was a woman named Etta Place with whom the Kid was romantically involved; she may have been either a schoolteacher or a prostitute.

Sundance was a feared gunman. While Butch was taught how to shoot by outlaw Mike Cassidy (whose last name he took), it is true that he never killed a man until he became a payroll guard in Bolivia. The reason they left the West for South America was because the law was closing in on them fast (Pinkerton detectives and railroad magnate E.H. Harriman's posse of "special employees"). Yet there was no actual chase and manhunt as described in the film.

Butch, Sundance and Etta did vacation in New York in 1902 before fleeing to South America. They ran a ranch in Argentina for a few years before riding the outlaw trail again. Etta returned to the United States in 1907. The two men were reported by Pinkerton agents to have been tracked down by Bolivian troops in 1909; the Kid was killed and Cassidy committed suicide. There were other accounts of their fate, including one that they survived, returned to the States and died quietly in 1937.

Writer William Goldman first became interested in their story in the late 1950s. After spending a number of years researching their lives, he wrote a first draft in 1966. There was both humor and poignancy in Goldman's script, and it was most winningly transferred to the screen by Hill, Newman and Redford.

Prior to its becoming a film, however, Goldman's scenario made the rounds of the various studios and its potential was not immediately recognized. It was even felt that the South American section should be eliminated in order to have the two outlaws stay in the West and fight the posse. Eventually, 20th Century–Fox's production head Richard D. Zanuck and vice-president of story operations David Brown bought Goldman's script for a then-record $400,000.

The writer envisioned Jack Lemmon as Butch Cassidy and Paul Newman as the Sundance Kid. While Zanuck liked Newman as Sundance, he wanted Steve McQueen for Butch. George Roy Hill preferred Robert Redford as Sundance and Paul as Butch. Zanuck balked at using Redford, who was not considered a big enough star at the time; even Newman initially saw the actor as "a Wall Street lawyer type." When McQueen expressed disinterest after learning that Newman would receive top billing, Zanuck and Brown wanted Marlon Brando. Any serious negotiation with Brando for Butch fell through, as did that with Warren Beatty for Sundance.

All this time, Hill held out for Redford, feeling he had the strength for the part; when the director finally convinced Newman, the actor forcefully rallied to Redford's side and convinced Zanuck. Seeing the terrific camaraderie between Redford and Newman during production, Zanuck admitted the error in his judgment. Not only did the two actors give unforgettable performances (among their very best), they also became the best of friends.

Paul Newman originally had some doubts about playing in another comedy as he was not very successful with the genre in the past. Hill convinced him that his part was not comic, only involved in humorous situations from time to time. The actor also took an active part in the film's production, having brought along a business partner, John Foreman, to function as producer. Paul Monash, 20th Century–Fox's initial choice to produce, was then made the executive producer.

In '56, Newman became a star playing boxer Rocky Graziano in MGM's drama *Somebody Up There Likes Me* (director, Robert Wise). The intense, rebellious streak in his acting was also seen in his first Western *The Left Handed Gun* (1958), in which he portrayed another legendary outlaw, Billy the Kid. Newman's talent for playing individualists at odds with society has served him well in many films, including *Hud* (Paramount, 1963), *The Outrage* (MGM, 1964) and *Hombre* (Fox, 1967). With four Oscar nominations then under his belt for Best Actor, he became the number one box office star in Hollywood in 1969 thanks largely to *Butch Cassidy and the Sundance Kid*.

While Robert Redford may have had the more aggressive role as Sundance, he never eclipsed Newman's more amiable playing as Butch. After the September release of the Western, Redford became an international celebrity like his already famous co-star. The appeal of their roles, notwithstanding their good looks and boyish humor, lies in Butch's good-naturedness and Sundance's physical grace.

Redford had made a promising film debut as a soldier in the 1962 drama *War Hunt* (United Artists; Denis Sanders, director). He gave a strong account of himself as a fugitive being tracked down by the ever-versatile Marlon Brando in a 1966 drama, *The Chase* (Columbia; Arthur Penn, director). But the actor was not very successful until he recreated his 1963 Broadway role of the newly-wed "lawyer" in 1967's comedy, *Barefoot in the Park* (Paramount; Gene Saks, director).

Also in 1967, Redford turned down Dustin Hoffman's role in another comedy called *The Graduate* (Embassy; Mike Nichols, director). It was a star-making role for Hoffman, who played a young man seduced by his girlfriend's mother; a blossoming young actress named Katharine Ross also became a star as the girlfriend. As Etta Place in *Butch Cassidy*, she fairly bloomed with a beautiful graciousness that only added to the film's luster.

The actress repeated her role in a 1976 ABC-TV movie, *Wanted: The Sundance Woman* (director, Lee Philips). Earlier, in '74, ABC aired the television movie *Mrs. Sundance* (director, Marvin Chomsky), starring Elizabeth Montgomery as Etta. The performances of the two ladies enhanced these average sequels. Fine performances from William Katt as Sundance and Tom Berenger as Butch were the best things about the big screen prequel *Butch and Sundance: The Early Days* (director Richard Lester, 1979).

In the original film, there were choice bits by any number of colorful supporting players, all who appear dumbfounded by the antics of Butch and Sundance: Strother Martin as Percy Garris, who stares with awe at the Kid's marksmanship; Jeff Corey as Bledsoe, who apologizes to the outlaws for envisioning a violent death for them; George Furth as Woodcock, who cannot help but like them even as they rob him; Kenneth Mars as the marshal, sorely tested trying to round up a posse; and the physically imposing Ted Cassidy as Harvey Logan, who, in one of the film's funniest moments, is kicked below the belt by Butch.

Filmed in the spring of '69, this Western cost $6,270,000 to make. Locations included terrain in Colorado (Durango, Silverton) and Utah (St. George, Grafton). Sites in Mexico (Cuernavaca, Taxco) substituted for South America. In California, the 20th Century–Fox studio and the Century Ranch at Malibu were also utilized. An Academy Award for Cinematography was given to Conrad Hall. The sepia tones opening and closing the film preserved the golden nostalgia of its Western time frame. An exquisite montage of stills (by John Neuhart and Lawrence Schiller), showing Etta, Sundance and Butch frolicking during their sojourn in New York, conveyed further the sentimental mood of the film's period in history.

Burt Bacharach's music, particularly the melancholy main theme, complemented the finely woven nostalgia. The Bacharach–Hal David song "Raindrops Keep Fallin' on My Head" is justifiably excused for being out of step with Butch and Etta's bicycle ride on a sunny morning simply because it is so much fun. Singer B.J. Thomas' rendition of the song was a big hit. Both song and score won Oscars, as did William Goldman's screenplay.

The script and the music score won out over *The Wild Bunch* that year. A contemporary drama about two social misfits, *Midnight Cowboy* (United Artists; John Schlesinger, director), won the Academy Award for Best Picture over *Butch Cassidy and the Sundance Kid*. Schlesinger won the Oscar for Best Director over George Roy Hill. The Western picked up a seventh Oscar nomination for Sound (William Edmundsen, David Dockendorf), but lost to the musical comedy, *Hello, Dolly!*

Despite the immense popularity of *Butch Cassidy and the Sundance Kid*, critics were not always appreciative of its numerous comedy elements. While the tale of outlaws in a 20th century West was told with more realism in *The Wild Bunch*, the latter film's hard edge and "R" rated violence kept it from being as appealing as Hill's film, which was given an "M" rating ("Suggested for mature audiences; parental discretion advised").

With more compassion than Peckinpah's film of unbridled passion, Hill and Goldman romantically mythologized their West and its outlaw heroes, who are attempting to embrace a world of their own. One of the film's great images is the so-called "superposse" chasing Butch and Sundance; for a time, only the sound of the outlaws' galloping horses are heard, as they ride into the Old West, folklore and our hearts.

Reviews

Saturday Review: "As Westerns go, it is extraordinarily good. William Goldman's script rings some witty changes on the ancient theme of banditry versus society, and the title roles are played with engaging skill by Paul Newman and Robert Redford."

Newsweek: "Hill, appreciating the attractiveness of his stars — including Katharine Ross as a proper, pristine gun moll — fills the wide screen with beautiful, gauzy color portraits."

I'd never really known who John Dunbar was—
perhaps the name itself had no meaning. But as
I heard my Sioux name being called over and
over, I knew for the first time who I really was.

KEVIN COSTNER *as John Dunbar/Dances with Wolves,*
reflecting after his Sioux tribe's victory
against the Pawnee raiders

Dances with Wolves

1990

Kevin Costner is invited into the Sioux camp; in time he will be honored as Dances with Wolves.

DANCES WITH WOLVES

A Tig Productions Presentation. Released by Orion Pictures, 1990. DeLuxe Color. Panavision. Orion Home Video. 181 minutes.

Credits: Kevin Costner (Director); Jim Wilson, Kevin Costner (Producers); Jake Eberts (Executive Producer); Bonnie Arnold (Associate Producer); Douglas C. Metzger, Stephen P. Dunn (Assistant Directors); John Huneck, Philip C. Pfeiffer (Second Unit Directors & Photographers); Michael Blake (Screenplay); Dean Semler (Photographer); Neil Travis (Editor); Jeffrey Beecroft (Production Designer); W. Ladd Skinner (Art Director); Lisa Dean (Set Decorator); Elsa Zamparelli (Costumes); Norman L. Howell (Stunts); John Barry (Music Score). Based on the novel by Michael Blake.

Cast: Kevin Costner (John Dunbar/Dances with Wolves); Mary McDonnell (Stands with a Fist); Graham Greene (Kicking Bird); Rodney A. Grant (Wind in His Hair); Floyd Red Crow Westerman (Ten Bears); Tantoo Cardinal (Black Shawl); Jimmy Herman (Stone Calf); Charles Rocket (Lt. Elgin); Robert Pastorelli (Timmons); Larry Joshua (Sgt. Bauer); Tony Pierce (Spivey); Tom Everett (Sgt. Pepper); Maury Chaykin (Major Fambrough); Nathan Lee Chasing His Horse (Smiles a Lot); Michael Spears (Otter); Jason R. Lone Hill (Worm); Doris Leader Charge (Pretty Shield); Kirk Baltz (Edwards); Wayne Grace (Major); Donald Hotton (General Tide); Annie Costner (Christine); Conor Duffy (Willie); Elisa Daniel (Christine's Mother); Percy White Plume (Big Warrior); John Tail (Escort Warrior); Steve Reevis (Sioux #1/Warrior #1); Sheldon Wolfchild (Sioux #2/Warrior #2); Wes Studi (Toughest Pawnee); Raymond Newholy (Sioux Courier); David J. Fuller (Kicking Bird's Son); Ryan White Bull (Kicking Bird's Eldest Son); Otakuye Conroy (Kicking Bird's Daughter); Maretta Big Crow (Village Mother); Steve Chambers (Guard); William H. Burton (General's Aide); Bill W. Curry (Confederate Cavalryman); Kent Hays (Wagon Driver); Robert Goldman (Union Soldier); Frank P. Costanza (Tucker); James A. Mitchell (Ray); R.L. Curtin (Ambush Wagon Driver); Nick Thompson, Carter Hanner (Confederate Soldiers); Buffalo Child, Clayton Big Eagle, Richard Leader Charge (Pawnees); Redwing Ted Nez, Marvin Holy (Sioux Warriors); Justin (Cisco); Teddy and Buck (Two Socks).

Synopsis

At St. David's Field, Tennessee, in 1863, Lt. John Dunbar, a Union soldier, lies with a foot wound during a Civil War battle. While the doctors contemplate whether to amputate, Dunbar forces his boot back on his injured foot and limps away. As the fight stalls between the Union and the Confederacy, Dunbar, in great pain and despair, wildly rides a horse past the enemy as they try to shoot him down. His comrades cheer him and he makes the suicide ride a second time with arms stretched out like Jesus on the cross. This inspires the other Yankees, and the Confederates are beaten back. In tribute to Dunbar's bravery, General Tide has a private surgeon attend to Dunbar's wound. He is also given a commission to journey to the Western frontier of his dreams with Cisco, the buckskin who carried him through the suicide run.

At Fort Hays in the Dakota Territory, Major Fambrough, who has apparently lost his mind from the isolation, gives Dunbar a charge at a farther outpost. He is to be taken there by a civilian supply driver named Timmons. Beginning their journey, John and Timmons hear a gunshot, not knowing the major has killed himself.

On the trail, John is enthralled by the beauty of the frontier, but he is irritated by Timmons' foul odor and behavior. At the outpost, Fort Sedgewick, John has to force Timmons at gunpoint to help unload the supplies because the place has been abandoned. After Timmons leaves, John finds in a creek the remains of animals killed by the fort's previous inhabitants. John burns the carcasses and then realizes that the smoke may attract Indians. A band of Pawnees see lingering smoke, but it turns out to be Timmons' campsite. Timmons is shot full of arrows and scalped.

John spots a friendly wolf whom he calls Two Socks. When John is bathing unseen in the creek, another Indian (not a Pawnee) tries to steal Cisco. But John surprises him, frightening the Indian away. Feeling the Indian will return with others, John buries some of the supply weapons as a precaution because Timmons had said that Indians are thieves.

The Indian who raced away from John is called Kicking Bird, and he is a Sioux medicine man. Kicking Bird tells his fellow tribesmen of the soldier's presence; several Sioux boys overhear this council and try to steal Cisco. John is knocked unconscious by the doorframe running after the children, but Cisco runs back to him anyway. A Sioux warrior, Wind in His Hair, also tries to steal the horse, which again gets away and returns to John.

Deciding to go see the Indians, John puts on his best uniform; Two Socks watches him ride away. En route he finds an injured Indian woman and carries her to the Sioux village. Neither John nor the Indians understand the other's language, but Wind in His Hair's attitude makes the soldier aware that he is not welcome.

Wind in His Hair and Kicking Bird are sent by Ten Bears, their chief, to learn why John is there at the fort. The language barrier is difficult to surmount, although John makes Kicking Bird understand his desire to see the buffalo. The Indians depend on the buffalo as they need them for food and clothing for the entire tribe. On a second visit, John gives the Indians coffee and sugar.

Stands with a Fist is the name of the woman John saved; she lives with Kicking Bird's family because her husband is dead. She is urged by Kicking Bird to communicate with John since she can speak his language, but she is afraid of being taken from her Sioux family. She is actually a white woman, raised as Kicking Bird's daughter after her frontier family was massacred by Pawnees when she was a child.

Kicking Bird gives John a buffalo hide, and the soldier is invited to the village. Stands with a Fist then acts as an interpreter.

While sleeping at the fort, John is awakened by an earthquake-like shaking. Running outside, he is overwhelmed to see a buffalo herd passing in the night. Ecstatic, he rushes to alert the Sioux. In the throes of a tribal ceremony, they almost harm John before he makes them understand about the buffalo.

Now looked upon with trust and acceptance, John journeys with the entire village on a three-day hunt. They find that some of the bison have apparently been killed by white hunters for the hides and tongues. Soon the tribe comes across the amazing sight of the whole herd. John joins the warriors in the exciting chase and kill; he also saves a young Indian, Smiles a Lot, from being crushed by a dangerous wounded animal.

That night there is a feast, and John is called upon time after time to tell of the day's adventure. When he returns to the fort, a terrible loneliness prevails and he acts out his own Indian dance around a campfire.

After a few days, John goes to visit his new friends; on the way, the Indians see him jumping around with Two Socks the wolf. John is honored with his own lodge amongst the Sioux, and he is also given an Indian name, Dances with Wolves.

When danger threatens the tribe from the Pawnees, Kicking Bird, Wind in His Hair and other Sioux warriors go after them. John, wishing to help in any fighting, is asked instead by Kicking Bird to watch over his family. Stands with a Fist tells John that this is a great honor. She and John spend a lot of time together; he learns from another Indian, Stone Calf, that her husband was killed and she is still in mourning. John writes in his journal that he loves her, and Two Socks finally trusts him enough to eat out of his hand. And Stands with a Fist returns John's love.

With the Sioux war party still away, the Pawnees sneak into the camp looking for blood. John's supply of guns, however, help the Sioux kill the Pawnee raiders. But Stone Calf is also killed in the struggle.

In time, John learns more and more of the Sioux language. Kicking Bird finds out from his wife Black Shawl that Stands with a Fist and John are in

Lt. John Dunbar (Kevin Costner, left) and the Sioux hunters watch the buffalo herd.

love. When the medicine man releases Stands with a Fist from her mourning, she and John have an Indian wedding.

When John relates to the Indians that many white people will come to their country, Ten Bears decides to take the tribe to the safer winter camp. John goes back to the fort to get his journal and finds a troop of soldiers there. Mistaking him for an Indian, the soldiers panic and kill Cisco. A soldier, Spivey, has found the journal but does not report it. John is beaten and put in chains, despite his contention that he is also a soldier. When John continues to be victimized, he tells the soldiers that his name is Dances with Wolves. While taking John back to Fort Hays as a traitor, an escort detachment kills Two Socks. Lt. Elgin stops the other soldiers from beating on John again.

Led by Wind in His Hair, Smiles a Lot and a party of Sioux braves rescue John and kill the soldiers. John's journal floats away in the river. The Sioux then return with John to their snowy camp. Stands with a Fist is waiting and rushes to her husband's arms.

Dances with Wolves realizes he must leave his friends because more soldiers will come to look for him; he must try to explain to the white people the things that have happened to him. After the snow breaks, he bids a last farewell to Kicking Bird, who can now speak English, and to Smiles a Lot, who has found his journal. He then rides away with Stands with a Fist at his side. From a mountain ledge, Wind in His Hair shouts his pledge of friendship to Dances with Wolves. By the time the soldiers find the campsite of the Indians, the entire tribe has gone.

Thirteen years later, the last of the free Sioux submit to the advancing white civilization.

While Western films from the 1960s, '70s and '80s focused on themes of parody and a changing West, they did so never realizing that audiences' interest in the genre was fading. This was no doubt helped along by these very parodies. This is not to say that the '70s or the '80s saw the death of the Western, for interest was sustained to a certain small degree. But the shine had dimmed from its once bright star.

In 1970, Sam Peckinpah looked again at the Old West in a changing time, albeit with a gentler approach, in Warner Bros.' *The Ballad of Cable Hogue*. The same year's *Monte Walsh* (National General; William A. Fraker, director) paid tribute to the final days of the cowboy. For a time in the 1970s and 1980s, it seemed as though the cowboy film had indeed seen its last days; audiences flocked to outer-space epics like *Star Wars* and the *Star Trek* films instead. Loaded with high-tech gimmickry, these films may have seemed more sophisticated than the Western genre, but in fact both Westerns and space operas were based on themes of good against evil.

The "Spaghetti Westerns" proved they were just a fad by the '70s, despite their continuing influence. Howard Hawks made his very last film a Western, 1970's *Rio Lobo* (National General), which was a nostalgic reworking of his *Rio Bravo* theme once more starring John Wayne.

During this decade, the Duke appeared in two especially noteworthy Westerns — 1972's *The Cowboys* (Warner Bros.; Mark Rydell, director), and 1976's *The Shootist* (Paramount; Don Siegel, director). The latter film, about a gunman living past his time into a modern West, was the actor's last. Joel McCrea made a nice little farewell Western in 1976, *Mustang Country* (Universal; John Champion, director). One year earlier, another Western great, Roy Rogers, starred in a modest film called *Mackintosh and T.J.* (Penland; director, Marvin J. Chomsky) — it was the "King of the Cowboys" first movie since he made a cameo as himself in the 1959 comedy Western *Alias Jesse James*. Rogers, of course, did enormously well with his television show in the '50s and when it was rerun during the first half of the '60s.

The two longest prime time Western series programs on television — *Bonanza* (#2 with 14½ years) and *Gunsmoke* (#1 with 20 seasons) — were taken off the air due to poor ratings in '73 and '75 respectively. James Arness, *Gunsmoke*'s legendary lawman Matt Dillon, took over the John Wayne role (and gave a strong performance) in an average television remake of *Red River* in 1988 (CBS; director, Richard Michaels). Prior to this last effort, in 1978 and 1979, two limited but epic series tried with above-average results to carry on the great tradition of television Westerns. The first, with Arness as head of the frontier family the Macahans, was ABC's *How the West Was Won* (inspired by the 1962 motion picture; its roster of directors included Burt Kennedy). The other, with an all-star cast involved in the growth of a town in Colorado, was NBC's *Centennial* (based on a James A. Michener novel).

In 1980, *Heaven's Gate* (United Artists; Michael Cimino, director) made a serious attempt to rejuvenate the big-screen Western epic with its historic theme of the Wyoming range wars of 1892. Two other fine historical Westerns were also released in 1980 — *The Long Riders* (United Artists; director, Walter Hill), and *Tom Horn* (Warner Bros.; director, William Wiard) — but all three films were unsuccessful at the box office. Nineteen eighty-one's *The Legend of the Lone Ranger* (Universal; William A. Fraker, director) was supposed to be another strong vehicle, yet it failed as well. (Lost here was the innocence of yesteryear which so mythologized the legendary "Masked Rider of the Plains" immortalized in his television heyday of the '50s by the unforgettable Clayton Moore.)

But a pair of outstanding Western epics — one on television, the other a motion picture — again made the call of the West truly irresistible. The first was CBS' 1989 mini-series *Lonesome Dove* (director, Simon Wincer). The second was *Dances with Wolves* in 1990.

The story of a massive cattle drive between Texas and Montana, and loaded with many dynamic characters and subplots (in the vein of *Centennial*), *Lonesome Dove* gave the network a tremendous lead in the ratings when it was televised over four consecutive nights. Between 1990 and 1991, *Dances with Wolves* amassed a domestic box office gross of $81,537,971, at the time surpassing the 1974 comedy oater *Blazing Saddles* (Warner Bros.; director, Mel Brooks) as the top moneymaking Western film. There was none of the slapstick humor of *Blazing Saddles*, nor the 26 hours of drama of *Centennial*, but both *Lonesome Dove* and *Dances with Wolves* were able to bring together a combination of realistic humor and drama never more appreciated in the Western realm.

The heritage of the American Indian has been told countless times on the silver screen, but was perhaps never touched upon so lovingly as in *Dances with Wolves*. It's true that many Western films highlighted the Indian as either a noble red man (1954's *Apache*) or murderous savages (1972's *Ulzana's Raid*). There was a common element in these films (and others): The Indian race striving for a life free from the white society violently bent on crushing their tribal cultural beliefs.

Sympathy for the Indian people, and the theme of a white man loving an Indian woman, as depicted in *Dances with Wolves*, were not new to films (although Stands with a Fist is really a Sioux-raised white woman). *Broken Arrow* was the big trailblazer 40 years earlier, with its focus on the Apache tribe and the ill-fated marriage between Indian maiden Sonseeahray (Debra Paget), and white scout Tom Jeffords (James Stewart). Cochise, the great Apache chief (Jeff Chandler), helped set the noble standard of quiet dignity and strength for Indian leadership in this film for other Westerns, including *Dances with Wolves*.

Other films which followed *Broken Arrow* with a similar theme of miscegenation included 1957's *Run of the Arrow* (RKO; Samuel Fuller, director) and 1970's *A Man Called Horse* (National General; Elliot Silverstein, director). The latter two Westerns even went so far as to show the violence inherent in the Sioux culture; *Dances with Wolves* does not do this to the same degree.

Explored with the utmost sensitivity in this later film is the Sioux way of life as a family unit. It must be added that, while this approach was wholly accepted by audiences, the movie does have a tendency to overdo the fellowship just as many earlier Westerns overdid their depiction of Indians as howling forces of evil. But the film should not be severely faulted for its generosity or for the self-indulgence of its director/producer/star Kevin Costner, simply because it is so beautifully mounted. The heartfelt depiction of Sioux life could not have been more thoughtfully presented.

With the white civilization advancing ever westward, the Sioux, like other Indian tribes, were eventually put on reservations and their culture seemed no longer their own. In 1868, the Sioux chose the Black Hills of Dakota as their land, free of all white settlers. The U.S. Government approved of this, but Lieutenant Colonel George Armstrong Custer led an expeditionary force of soldiers into this part of the country in 1874. Word spread that gold was discovered there and miners came into the sacred Indian land; the Sioux retaliated by attacking the white people. General Philip H. Sheridan tried to keep the pledge made to the Indians, but settlers refused to pull out. The conflicts continued and, in 1876, Custer disobeyed orders and with 215 soldiers attacked the Indians at the Little Bighorn River in Montana. A body of well over 1,000

Sioux and Cheyenne warriors had formed, and Custer and his men were wiped out.

Sitting Bull and Crazy Horse were two of the dominant Sioux chiefs involved in the Battle of the Little Bighorn. A year later, Crazy Horse was forced to return to the reservation with his hungry tribe because of the dwindling numbers of buffalo; he was killed there by guards while resisting arrest. In 1881, Sitting Bull was also forced by the U.S. Army onto a reservation with his starving people — there the Indians began the famous "Ghost Dance," where they would seek solace by retreating into a spirit world with their loved ones returning from the dead, and with the land once more full of buffalo. The army tried to stop the "Ghost Dance" by 1890, and Sitting Bull was killed in the struggle.

The story of Custer's Last Stand has been a part of many motion pictures — he was glorified as a hero in 1941's *They Died with Their Boots On*, and he was a despicable fool in 1970's *Little Big Man* among other entries. In early 1991, just a few months after the November '90 release of *Dances with Wolves*, an ABC mini-series, *Son of the Morning Star*, was televised in two parts. Although a major production, directed by Mike Robe, it failed to generate much audience response; it attempted to present a historical perspective on the proud and arrogant Custer. Ironically, after filming his first Western in 1985, *Silverado* (Columbia; Lawrence Kasdan, director), Kevin Costner was interested in doing the Custer saga when it was initially presented to NBC. But the network turned the project down, partly because the actor was not then "a big enough star."

The rise of Kevin Costner as a weighty filmmaker would prove phenomenal. The unbelievable success he enjoyed with *Dances with Wolves* came about because of the creation of his own production company in 1989 (Tig) with fellow producer and friend Jim Wilson. The two men and writer Michael Blake had originally worked together on a 1983 gambling drama, *Stacy's Knights* — Wilson as director and an executive producer, Blake as screenwriter and Costner in his first leading role.

Another filmmaker, Lawrence Kasdan, had cut Kevin's part from the 1983 drama, *The Big Chill* (in which he is now seen only as a corpse). Consequently the director felt compelled to give the actor a part in another picture. Thus, Kevin was cast in *Silverado*. His flamboyant gunslinger Jake was a delightful throwback to the old-time heroes of both Western and swashbuckling films; and it certainly put him on the trail to stardom.

In fact, Costner's screen personality, sensitive, rugged, and, above all, quietly determined, was given its due in films following *Silverado*. He became a full-fledged star as crime fighter Eliot Ness in 1987's gangster drama *The Untouchables* (Paramount; director, Brian DePalma) and fortified his stardom with, among others, the 1989 fantasy film *Field of Dreams* (Universal; director, Phil Alden Robinson). With his success assured, Costner was able to exceed his own expectations when Tig Productions was formed and signed with Orion Pictures to distribute *Dances with Wolves*.

As early as 1986, Michael Blake was advised by Kevin to write a novel for consideration as a source for a possible screenplay. Costner loved Blake's novel *Dances with Wolves* immediately because of the story's romantic look at a past American culture, one felt to have suffered greatly in the name of progress. Blake was assigned to write the screenplay and kept the script faithful to the novel's spirit. However, as with most books turned into films, the 1988 novel has many additions and differences compared to the 1990 film.

In the book, a Captain Cargill marches back to Fort Hays from Fort Sedgewick with 18 soldiers, unseen by Timmons and Dunbar; Cargill also learns that Major Fambrough has been sent back East after losing his mind. (The major does not kill himself as in the film). In the novel, the Civil War battle takes place in Pennsylvania instead of Tennessee, and the conflict is mentioned when Dunbar is in his second night at Fort Sedgewick. In the film, the Civil War episode is the opening sequence. The novel opens with Dunbar and Timmons en route to Fort Sedgewick, and on the journey there is a reference to the lieutenant being given the post by Fambrough.

The novel refers to the Indians as Comanches, not the Sioux tribe in the film. Both Kicking Bird and Ten Bears have more than one wife in the book, and Stands with a Fist has lost two babies with her own Comanche husband. During the course of Blake's novel, her husband is killed while fighting Ute Indians; she then attempts suicide, but is stopped by the Comanche women. When Dunbar then finds her, Stands with a Fist is weak from losing too much blood, having cut herself as a tribute to her dead husband. In the film, he is already dead, there is no mention of any children lost, and it is left unclear why she is hurt when John finds her.

When Dunbar and a group of Comanches find some of the buffalo slaughtered by white hunters in the book, the soldier later learns that the hunters were killed and scalped by the Indians. The novel has no dramatic rescue by Dunbar during the buffalo chase, and Stone Calf survives the fight with the Pawnees.

In the novel, Dances with Wolves has very little to give as presents to Kicking Bird for allowing him to marry Stands with a Fist, and the tribe contributes over 20 horses in his behalf. Also in the book but not the film is a segment in which Dances with Wolves is shown a sacred forest for the creation of all the wildlife; he and Kicking Bear are appalled to find the abandoned camp of white men who have mutilated dozens of animal corpses.

Both Kicking Bird and Stone Calf are with Wind in His Hair when

Dances with Wolves is rescued from the soldiers in the novel; as in the film, he then believes he should leave the tribe lest more soldiers come. Both sources relate how Ten Bears tells Dances with Wolves that the soldiers will be seeking one of their own and not an Indian warrior. It is assumed because there are then no farewells in the book that he does stay.

It should be mentioned that another book, *Dances with Wolves, The Illustrated Story of the Epic Film* by Costner, Blake and Wilson, reveals that certain filmed scenes were omitted from the three-hour movie — the abandonment of Sedgewick by Cargill and his men; Stands with a Fist grieving over the dead body of her Sioux husband; the killing of the white buffalo hunters; the Sioux village donating gifts on behalf of Dances with Wolves; and the journey to the sacred forest, among others. An additional 50 minutes or so of footage conveying these omissions were included in the film's network television world premiere in 1993. Orion Home Video subsequently released a 237-minute version (with the restored footage), giving admirers of the film their choice of the original or the longer video.

The Indians were changed from Comanche to Sioux in the film because South Dakota was chosen as a location. Not only was the Dakota Territory Sioux country during the 1860s (as a state it still remains their homeland), but the biggest buffalo herd in the world was found there — some 3,500 animals privately owned by rancher Roy Houck. The producers felt they needed a massive herd to fully convey the awesome spectacle of a time when thousands upon thousands of the animals roamed the West in great herds.

Three thousand of the rancher's herd were used in the film's greatest sequence of thrilling and breathtaking wonder. In eight days, 60,000 feet of buffalo hunt footage was shot, but just four minutes of it reached the screen. Twenty-four artificial buffalo made of wire, polyurethane and fur appeared as the dead and skinned beasts; they were supplied by the special effects firm of Kurtzman, Nicotero and Berger in Chatsworth, California.

From Indian reservations in South Dakota, including Pine Ridge and Rosebud, 250 Sioux were hired as extras. Subtitles were seen when the actual Sioux dialect Lakota was spoken. Doris Leader Charge, a teacher at Rosebud's Sinte Gleska College, translated the screenplay's Indian dialogue; she also coached many of the cast members and played the part of Pretty Shield, the wife of Ten Bears. Other real Sioux in the movie included Floyd Red Crow Westerman as this wise old chief and Nathan Lee Chasing His Horse as the young Smiles a Lot.

Two of the most charismatic figures in the film are Rodney A. Grant's Wind in His Hair and Graham Greene's Kicking Bird. Grant, an Omaha Indian, and Greene, an Oneida Indian, perfectly embodied the mystique, dignity and graciousness of the noblest movie Indians ever seen. But the film's true romantic heart belongs to Mary McDonnell's Stands with a Fist and Kevin Costner's John Dunbar/Dances with Wolves. Their love is the bridge between two cultures, thus representing the entire soul of the story despite any loose ends in continuity. Every performance is a standout.

Dances with Wolves was nominated for 12 Academy Awards and won seven. It was the first Western since 1930–31's *Cimarron* to be chosen for Best Picture. For his directorial debut, Costner won another Oscar; he was nominated for a third as Best Actor, losing to Jeremy Irons in *Reversal of Fortune*. Nominated as Best Supporting Actor, Graham Greene lost to Joe Pesci in *Good-Fellas*; Mary McDonnell lost her Best Supporting Actress nod to Whoopi Goldberg in *Ghost*. Michael Blake won the Oscar for Writing — Screenplay Based on Material from Another Medium. Dean Semler was given the statuette for Cinematography.

Given an Oscar nomination for Art Direction-Set Decoration, Jeffrey Beecroft and Lisa Dean lost to Richard Sylbert and Rick Simpson for *Dick Tracy*. Elsa Zamparelli was nominated for Costume Design (her Indian costumes are exquisite), but Franca Squarciapino won for *Cyrano de Bergerac*. The Western won its final three Oscars for Original Score (John Barry); Film Editing (Neil Travis) and Sound (Russell Williams II, Jeffrey Perkins, Bill W. Benton, Greg Watkins).

With approximately a 17-week, $21,000,000 shooting schedule, *Dances with Wolves* certainly was an epic of the highest order — that it succeeded, at a time when Westerns were not at their most popular, was extraordinary. It had a feeling for landscapes and people that John Ford might have envied; another key to its success was Kevin Costner's enthusiasm as a filmmaker. The innocence of the character he plays is in complete harmony with the film's sensitivity. As a novice director, he more fully captures his Indian saga's idealism and romanticism than does Ford's final tribute to the American Indian *Cheyenne Autumn* (1964), an epic tale of several hundred Indians' trek back to their homeland after fleeing a reservation.

Reviews

Variety: "Costner's directing style is fresh and assured. A sense of surprise and humor accompany Dunbar's adventures at every turn, twisting the narrative gently this way and that and making the journey a real pleasure."

Newsweek: "*Dances with Wolves* is vulnerable both to charges of sentimentality and anachronism — the hero exhibits a sensibility at times dubiously contemporary. But if one's mind sometimes balks, one's heart embraces the movie's fine, wide-open spirit, its genuine respect for a culture we destroyed without a second thought."

*It's a helluva thing killin' a man. You take away
all he's got, and all he's ever gonna have.*

CLINT EASTWOOD *as William Munny*

Unforgiven

1992

Clint Eastwood (left) and Morgan Freeman.

UNFORGIVEN

A Malpaso Production. A Warner Brothers Presentation, 1992. Technicolor. Panavision. Warner Home Video. 131 minutes.

Credits: Clint Eastwood (Director and Producer); David Valdes (Executive Producer); Julian Ludwig (Associate Producer); Scott Maitland (First Assistant Director); David Webb Peoples (Screenplay); Jack N. Green (Photographer); Joel Cox (Editor); Henry Bumstead (Production Designer); Rick Roberts, Adrian Gorton (Art Directors); Janice Blackie-Goodine (Set Decorator); James J. Murakami (Set Designer); Mike Hancock (Makeup); Lennie Niehaus (Music Score).

Cast: Clint Eastwood (William Munny); Gene Hackman (Little Bill Daggett); Morgan Freeman (Ned Logan); Richard Harris (English Bob); Jaimz Woolvett (The "Schofield Kid"); Saul Rubinek (W.W. Beauchamp); Frances Fisher (Strawberry Alice); Anna Thomson (Delilah Fitzgerald); David Mucci (Quick Mike); Rob Campbell (Davey Bunting); Anthony James (Skinny Dubois); Shane Meier (Will Munny); Aline Levasseur (Penny Munny); Tara Dawn Frederick (Little Sue); Beverley Elliott (Silky); Liisa Repo-Martell (Faith); Josie Smith (Crow Creek Kate); Cherrilene Cardinal (Sally Two Trees).

Synopsis

In 1878, William Munny buries his wife after she dies from smallpox. Her mother never could understand why she married a reputed outlaw.

Two years later, in Big Whiskey, Wyoming, a pair of cowboys are involved in a scuffle in the local brothel with Delilah, a prostitute; the woman's face is badly cut by the knife of the older man. Skinny Dubois, the brothel's owner, stops the fight at gunpoint. Sheriff Little Bill Daggett and his deputies are then brought to the scene.

Daggett is set to whip the cowboys, yet relents after listening to Skinny's claim that Delilah is now damaged goods. Instead, Daggett orders the cowboys to bring in a string of ponies to Skinny (later, the younger cowboy offers Delilah the prize pony). But the other prostitutes led by their madam, Strawberry Alice, are so infuriated by this injustice that they go behind the sheriff's back and take up a collection of $1,000 to hire gunmen to shoot the cowboys.

A young, self-proclaimed gunfighter, the "Schofield Kid," turns up on Will Munny's Kansas pig farm to convince him to help go after the cowboys;

the kid has heard of the older man's reputation as a killer. However, Will is not responsive to the notion of killing anymore. He admits to having been influenced by whiskey when he brandished a gun during his deadly past, and says that he gave up his lawless ways thanks to the influence of his late wife. Will's life is now spent working his farm and raising two children, little Will and Penny. The Kid rides out alone.

Tired of struggling with his poor farm, Will decides to follow after the Kid, even though he has trouble shooting with a pistol and mounting his frisky horse. Will leaves the children behind, reassuring them that he will return in two weeks. He tells them to go to neighbor Ned Logan's Indian companion Sally Two Trees if they need any help while he's gone.

Stopping off at Ned's place, Will convinces his old partner to accompany him, partake in the killings and share the money with the "Schofield Kid." Will tells Ned that with his share, he plans to give his son and daughter a better life.

When the two men catch up to the Kid and he begins firing wildly at them, they realize the younger man cannot see 50 yards. The Kid is against splitting the money a third way, but he relents when Will refuses to go without Ned. On the trail, the Kid brags on how many men he has killed.

Another gunman who has heard about the cash bounty and is bound for Big Whiskey is a colorful railroad worker called English Bob. Traveling with him is writer W.W. Beauchamp, who has turned the gunfighter's exploits into a dime novel. In Big Whiskey, English Bob is informed by one of Little Bill's deputies that a town ordinance bans carrying firearms; although he is clearly displaying a handgun, the gunman lies to the deputy. Before long, English Bob and Beauchamp are confronted by Sheriff Daggett. The lawman forces Bob to hand over two pistols and, as a warning to other gunmen, then beats him to a bloody pulp with the townsfolk watching.

Beauchamp is thrown in jail with Bob, but his writing intrigues Little Bill enough to set the writer free. After busting the myth about one of English Bob's past heroics (where he had actually shot an unarmed man), the sheriff's own background becomes of interest to Beauchamp. The gunfighter is forced to leave town.

Newly arrived in Big Whiskey and feeling feverish, Will stays in the saloon while the Kid and Ned are in the upstairs brothel with the prostitutes. While tending to a leaky roof and trying to relate his past feats of heroism to Beauchamp, Little Bill receives word about the three strangers in town.

Approached by Daggett and his deputies, Will lies that he is not carrying a gun. He, too, is beaten badly by the sheriff before being allowed to crawl out of the saloon and into a rain-soaked, muddy street. Ned and the Kid follow, having escaped the lawman's wrath.

Will recovers from his fever and beating in a secluded area outside of town. Helping him through his ordeal, Delilah finds Will to be sympathetic to her own misfortune; his memories of his wife, however, prevent Will from doing anything more intimate. He does assure her that they still plan to kill the cowboys. In fact, both the Kid and Ned have been sharing two of the prostitutes' sexual favors as an advance towards their payment for the killings.

Finding one of the cowboys, Davey Bunting, rounding up stray cattle, Ned shoots the man's horse out from under him. But Ned quickly realizes that he does not have the stomach for killing anymore. Instead, Will fires three shots at the cowboy, the last one proving fatal. Ned decides to return home, but he is captured and taken to Little Bill. Accusing him of being an assassin, the sheriff whips Ned.

Not knowing of their friend's predicament, the Kid and Will trail the other cowboy, Quick Mike, to his bunkhouse. At close range, the Kid shoots the man dead in the outhouse.

One of the prostitutes brings the two men their bounty money as the Kid, disturbed by having killed a man, confesses that it was actually the first time. Will begins drinking whiskey when told by the prostitute that Little Bill, upon hearing of the second cowboy's murder, killed Ned. The Kid is afraid of Will's hard new countenance, but Will assures his friend that he will not harm him.

Will tells the "Schofield Kid" to take his share of the money to his (Will's) children, as he finishes the whiskey bottle and confronts the sheriff in the Big Whiskey saloon. He shoots an unarmed Skinny, then kills some of the deputies and Little Bill. Beauchamp tries to approach Will about the stratagem of a gunfighter; the writer, taken aback when his life is threatened, runs off. Will threatens to kill anyone who tries to stop him from leaving town or who bothers the prostitutes. With the townspeople staring after him, Will rides away into the night.

Will Munny pays his respects at his wife's grave. Her mother later came to pay her respects as well, but found Will and the children long gone. She never knew why her daughter had married an outlaw.

The first American writer of international repute, James Fenimore Cooper immortalized the heroic frontiersman in his series of *Leather-Stocking Tales* written in the 19th century. Cooper's most famous story was 1826's *The Last of the Mohicans*; its protagonist, Natty Bumppo, a white man raised amongst Indians, has all the attributes of the traditional frontier heroes of literature and film — courage, loyalty and, of course, a ferocity with a gun. So revered is this

Clint Eastwood and Anna Thomson.

particular frontiersman with a long rifle that he is called Hawkeye. Perhaps the first noted gunfighter was thus born, plying his skill killing those miscreants who would endanger others. A fourth sound version of this epic adventure and romance (from 20th Century–Fox; director, Michael Mann) was released in 1992, the same year as *Unforgiven*.

The noble figure of Hawkeye is an ancestor of many future Western gunmen, notably Shane. Despite the nobility of Shane, however, he realized all too well that once you have killed, you are branded a killer. The 1953 film *Shane* showed how the gunfighter taint affected two of its characters, one good and the other evil. While there were other Westerns that showed the combination of good and bad traits in gunmen, it was not until *Unforgiven*, almost 40 years after *Shane*, that the complex nature of the gunfighter was again explored so successfully. Where *Shane* mythologized elements in the Western genre, *Unforgiven* demythologized them. At the same time, it remained faithful to the spirit of the gunman embraced over the years by its star, Clint Eastwood.

The legend of Eastwood is second only to John Wayne; both are monumental figures in the history of Western films. Like Wayne, Eastwood became a major film star via the Western. Unlike Wayne, he first attracted serious attention in television, scoring a long run on CBS's series *Rawhide* between 1959 and 1966, playing a good-natured and heroic cowboy named Rowdy

Yates. This series, about many cattle drives, drew its inspiration from 1948's *Red River*. In 1964, Clint also starred in the Italian Western *A Fistful of Dollars* for director Sergio Leone. The actor's screen personality was born in this film with his portrayal of a bounty hunter called The Man with No Name — stoic to the point of being a cool, mysterious loner; ruthless to the extreme of not being particular what man was in his deadly gunsight for a cash reward; and tinged with a trace of nobility for his fearlessness and for following his own sense of morality.

His bounty hunter first made him famous in Europe. As an anti-hero, Eastwood proved irresistible to audiences — he was in sequels for Leone in '65 (*For a Few Dollars More*) and in '66 (*The Good, the Bad and the Ugly*). After the trilogy was released by United Artists in America during the late '60s, he gained international acclaim. These "Spaghetti Westerns" were a brutal depiction of a cruel land and crueller men and indeed demythologized the Old West as set forth in many American films. It was sometimes hard to separate Eastwood's hero from that of a villain.

Clint Eastwood would make his patented gunman into a tremendous part of his big screen success. Having formed his own production company, Malpaso, in 1968, his initial film for this outfit was another violent Western, *Hang 'Em High* (director, Ted Post). It was Eastwood's first American film as a star, and the violence was certainly influenced by the aforementioned Italian Westerns. Also in '68, his contemporary Western hero in Universal's *Coogan's Bluff* began a long association with its producer/director Don Siegel. This duo's most famous entry was 1971's crime thriller *Dirty Harry* (for Warner Brothers/Seven Arts). As the rebel detective Harry Callahan, Clint was a modern variant of the indomitable Westerner that he had played and would continue to play over the years.

Siegel and Eastwood teamed in '70 for their first Old West saga, *Two Mules for Sister Sara*. In '72 and '73 respectively, Eastwood made the Westerns *Joe Kidd* (with John Sturges directing) and *High Plains Drifter* (which he directed himself). As The Stranger in the latter film, Eastwood's mysterious rider, who may be an avenging ghost, pays homage to his Man with No Name persona.

Until *Unforgiven*, Clint's best Western was 1976's epic *The Outlaw Josey Wales*, which he also directed. In this earlier film's title role, he played a character, much like the one in *High Plains Drifter*, on the trail of vengeance. But Josey Wales is a richer role in its depth of vulnerability and humanity. Eastwood entered the 1980s with more vulnerable screen roles (his characters had more flaws in their nature); and this was evident in the Western character of 1980's *Bronco Billy*. Like *Coogan's Bluff*, this latter film is not a true Western in period setting or story, but it contains one of the gentlest of the actor's performances.

Clint's most humane Westerner may be the Preacher in 1985's *Pale Rider*, who is once more a mysterious presence (perhaps another ghost rider), and comes to the aid of a community of miners up against an evil business interest. The film resembled *Shane* in many scenes; however, the violence was far more savage than the pioneering sequence of brutal gunplay where Jack Palance's gunman blows away Elisha Cook, Jr.'s farmer.

From 1976 to 1992, Eastwood was the director of all his Westerns; for *Bronco Billy, Pale Rider* and *Unforgiven*, he was also credited as producer. His performance in the latter film is assuredly the most fully developed one in regards to its violent nature. The character of Will Munny was an infamous gunman and, like the Man with No Name, used his gun for profit. He becomes like the vengeful *High Plains Drifter*— the complexity of the role lies with the metamorphosis of the gunman, who is disturbed by what he once was and actually becomes feverish before turning again into a killer. He redeems himself by being loyal to a friend unjustly killed by a brutally tough lawman.

Toughness seems to be the requisite for survival (the tougher, the better the chances) in the harsh West of *Unforgiven*, where both bad and good traits are part of each man and woman. But most everyone seems to be a victim. Gene Hackman's Sheriff Little Bill Daggett has his own code of tough morality just as Munny has — the lawman's brutality overpowers Richard Harris' showy English Bob and Eastwood's gunman at first, but he finally succumbs when the latter gunfighter reveals a fiercer nature. Even the prostitutes, especially their leader Strawberry Alice (Frances Fisher) and the disfigured Delilah (Anna Thomson) react with their own unforgiving sense of frontier justice by calling in the gunmen. Jaimz Woolvett as the "Schofield Kid" feigns toughness with a gun — his revulsion at killing one man turns to fear of the hardened Munny (who then confirms his friendship for the Kid, as he would later to his dead comrade Ned). Morgan Freeman's Ned loses his life because he is not tough enough to kill anymore; when his only desire is to return home, he is branded a killer and whipped to death by the sheriff.

Little Bill loses his own life to Munny because originally he was not tough enough to punish with severity the two cowboys who hurt Delilah. Even though there is justice in that they are punished for scarring Delilah, the killing of the cowboys by Munny and the Kid is a deplorable act of double murder. That Little Bill is tough enough to reciprocate by murdering Ned only reinforces Will's killing instincts. By the time he rides off, having exacted his own tough frontier justice, the eternal Clint Eastwood avenger has returned.

The darkness of the night serves as a grim reminder of the darker nature of many a Western film with revisionist overtones. *Unforgiven* also serves as a vehicle for two of the most powerful performances from its leading players, Eastwood and Gene Hackman.

Eastwood would be nominated for an Academy Award as Best Actor and Hackman would win the Oscar and a New York Film Critics Award as Best Supporting Actor. Always able to inject into his roles their fullest human dimensions, Hackman shows his facility in *Unforgiven* with the good humor he has for Skinny, Beauchamp and the deputies, and a sadistic nature against any transgressors which questions his professionalism as a lawman. Hackman had already won an Oscar as Best Actor for his brusque law enforcer in 1971's crime thriller, *The French Connection*. His last Western motion picture before *Unforgiven* was 1975's *Bite the Bullet,* yet his natural affinity as an actor made it seem like he had been riding in the saddle for years.

Like Hackman, Morgan Freeman is called one of America's greatest actors. A major influence in the American theater prior to his big screen successes in the late 1980s, he duplicated his 1987 success in Alfred Uhry's stage play *Driving Miss Daisy* in the 1989 film version of the drama. Freeman's Ned Logan is generally a placid character as compared to Daggett and Munny, but more humane because of his realization that he cannot cope with the inherent violence. His death provides Will with a chance for salvation; Ned is the most sympathetic role in the film.

One performer who (like Eastwood) had appeared in several previous Western films was Richard Harris. Among his more notable Westerns were *Major Dundee* in 1965 and the trilogy of *Man Called Horse* films (1970, 1976 and 1984 respectively). His effervescent personality seemed perfect for the small but colorful role of English Bob. He also is a sympathetic character. The viciousness of Little Bill is first exhibited in this gunman's beating; the violence here is a total shock as the sheriff had only shown an indifference toward the prostitutes. While there is also a trace of sympathy in the film for the cowboys (particularly Rob Campbell's Davey Bunting), the gunmen have the edge in this light.

Anna Thomson and Frances Fisher convey the timeless plight of women deemed unworthy. The quiet, tender moments that Will shares with Delilah, extending to her some compassion, are among the film's most poignant.

Newcomer Jaimz Woolvett holds his own amongst the seasoned troupers. The "Schofield Kid," nicknamed after the type of gun he holsters, is representative of the many trigger-happy young guns roaming the West in countless films (like, for instance, Billy the Kid). Fortunately, the young man in *Unforgiven* discovers that he is no gun hand and is able to ride away from a confrontation with the sheriff. Not so with Billy — in 1881 New Mexico, his killing ways caught up to him when he was shot dead by Sheriff Pat Garrett.

Unfortunately, the film's Ned Logan ends up being killed as had many actual outlaws in the Old West. Like Logan, Ned Huddleston was a black man who gave up, and then returned, to his lawless ways (under the name of Isom

Dart); in 1900 Wyoming, he was shot and killed for rustling, supposedly by Tom Horn. Sometimes an outlaw's own gang member shot him for the reward; such was the case in 1882 Missouri when Bob Ford killed Jesse James.

Certainly many men and women who were part of the Western experience knew each other, and some were even romantically linked, like Calamity Jane and Wild Bill Hickok. Born Martha Jane Cannary, Calamity came West with her mother and father in 1865. However, she lost her folks within the next two years, and was then known to frequent saloons supporting herself as a prostitute. She learned that to survive in the Wild West she had to become as tough as the best or worst of frontiersmen. Calamity developed an unrequited love for Wild Bill. She became a true heroine in 1878 (the year of the opening scene in *Unforgiven*) by helping smallpox victims in Deadwood, South Dakota. Hickok, a notorious gunman in his own right, was shot dead by Jack McCall in Deadwood two years earlier. Claiming to be his widow, Calamity Jane was buried beside him in 1903.

David Webb Peoples first wrote the script for *Unforgiven* 18 years before the film was actually made. Clint Eastwood bought the property for Malpaso eight years later and, while waiting for the right time to do it, made some attempt at changing the scenario. Ultimately, he realized that he loved the story as originally written.

Eastwood is phenomenal for bringing his films in under budget and on schedule. He did so admirably with *Unforgiven*. Filmed partially in Alberta, Canada, and Sonora, California, the landscapes (photographed by Jack N. Green), have a natural, poetic beauty. The focus was particularly on production designer Henry Bumstead's Western town and its conveyance of a dark, claustrophobic intimacy. Eastwood undoubtedly wanted this community's tragedies to reflect an anti-violent outlook.

The editing was tight and lean, and Joel Cox won an Academy Award for his work in this category. Bumstead and Janice Blackie-Goodine earned an Oscar nomination for Art Direction-Set Decoration, but lost the award to Luciana Arrighi and Ian Whittaker for *Howards End*. Nominated for Cinematography, Green lost to Philippe Rousselot for *A River Runs Through It*. For Screenplay Written Directly for the Screen, Peoples lost to Neil Jordan for *The Crying Game*. An Oscar nomination was given for Sound (Les Fresholtz, Vern Poore, Dick Alexander and Rob Young), but the award went to *The Last of the Mohicans*.

Eastwood lost his Best Actor nod to Al Pacino, star of *Scent of a Woman*, but he did win Oscars for Best Director and for producer when the film took the Best Picture honor. *Unforgiven* was only the third Western to win the top Oscar since the first Academy Awards ceremony in May 1929.

In the history of the American cinema, perhaps no two Westerns have been as prestigious as *Dances with Wolves* and *Unforgiven*. Kevin Costner and Clint Eastwood were both honored by the Directors Guild of America (in '90 and '92 respectively) for these films. Eastwood's R-rated Western won four of its nine Oscar nominations; Costner's PG-rated epic won three more than that.

Between its August '92 release and the March '93 Oscar ceremonies, *Unforgiven* had nudged past *Dances with Wolves* domestically at the box office, with earnings of $81,961,812. However, by March '96, *Variety*'s domestic "All-time B.O. List" had the Costner film down as the #1 Western (with $184,208,848). Behind 1974's *Blazing Saddles* and 1994's *Maverick* came Clint's film (with $101,157,447). The #5 Western on the list was *Butch Cassidy and the Sundance Kid* (with $96,681,900).

Another great interpretation of the Old West, *Unforgiven* proved that the Western film has come a long way from the old-fashioned simplicity and even sentiment of the pioneering efforts of John Ford. Yet Ford's later films, *The Searchers* (with a psychological twist to the anti-hero) and *The Man Who Shot Liberty Valance* (with a bittersweet feeling for a time and people) are comparable to the Eastwood Western. Ford, more than any other filmmaker, redefined the Western genre, just as Eastwood has done since '64 (ironically the year that John Ford made his final Western, *Cheyenne Autumn*).

Ethan Edwards and Chief Scar of *The Searchers* and Tom Doniphon and Liberty Valance from *The Man Who Shot Liberty Valance* are leaders not above reproach for killing. Will Munny and Little Bill Daggett are cut from the same cloth, men whose leadership contains violent fallibilities, stemming from their determination to live by their own standards, whether right or wrong. The violence that is part of their human nature manifests itself in the rawest form through the Western wilderness. The landscapes of the American West, beautiful yet brutal, are reflective of these hard men. Clint Eastwood and John Wayne in particular have developed screen personas of weathered, leathery endurance.

Every filmmaker, every performer, who has contributed to the genre, to the screen image of the flawed yet tough Western man, deserves recognition. Whether it has been Wayne or Eastwood, Cooper or Ladd, Lancaster or Douglas, Brynner or McQueen, McCrea or Scott, Fonda or Stewart, Widmark or Holden, Hackman or Costner or any of the others who have and who will ride the Western trail, their romantic allure is eternal.

Beginning in 1987, James Arness returned to form, thus keeping the flame burning, in a recurring string of Matt Dillon/*Gunsmoke* television movies on CBS. Also on CBS was James Garner in the 1995 mini-series, *Streets of Laredo* (director, Joseph Sargent), the "authorized" sequel to writer Larry McMurtry's earlier story *Lonesome Dove*. As the gritty ex-Texas ranger, Captain Woodrow

Call, Garner was in equally fine form. Garner, incidentally, was also in 1994's big screen version of *Maverick* (Warner Brothers; Richard Donner, director), although Mel Gibson took over the Bret Maverick role made famous by his co-star.

While Eastwood in *Unforgiven* and Garner in *Streets of Laredo* demythologize the Western genre with the shocking violent nature and all-too-human failings of their respective characters, they do not fail to add to the romanticism of rugged individualism. Both of these Westerns eclipse these individualists, however, with a stronger and more sentimental theme — that of family unity. It is Will's misguided quest to kill the cowboys that ultimately provides a better life with his son and daughter. And it is Call's quest, tracking down a young outlaw, that brings him a more fulfilled life as a foster father to the man's orphaned little sister.

In the last scene of *Unforgiven*, when Will Munny has returned to his wife's grave to say goodbye, there certainly is a more complete appreciation of the Western psyche. Under Eastwood's assured direction in this closing moment, Jack N. Green's lovely camerawork and Lennie Niehaus' equally lovely music score radiate a tenderness in the tradition of films like *Ride the High Country*, *The Searchers* and *Shane*.

While every great Western film has been a personal interpretation of the American past, there is a degree of realism, of truth, in the embodiment of the spirit of the Old West in all of them. For the most part, the genre has cast a melancholic reflection on the West and depicted the conflict between man's noble and savage instincts. Never lost is the haunting nostalgia that allows those who open their hearts to embrace the Western vision time and time again.

Reviews

Variety: "Playing a stubbly, worn-out, has-been outlaw who can barely mount his horse at first, Eastwood, unafraid to show his age, is outstanding in his best clipped, understated manner."

Newsweek: "He's disturbingly human in *Unforgiven*, a stunning, dark Western that may stand as actor/director Eastwood's summation of the form. It's a classical tale of the Old West that's a radical critique of Western movie conventions."

BIBLIOGRAPHY

Anderson, Lindsay. *About John Ford*. New York: McGraw-Hill, 1981.

Anobile, Richard J., ed. *Stagecoach*. New York: Darien House/Universe, 1975.

Arce, Hector. *Gary Cooper: An Intimate Biography*. New York: Morrow, 1979.

Balio, Tino. *United Artists: The Company Built by the Stars*. Madison: University of Wisconsin Press, 1976.

_____. *United Artists: The Company That Changed the Film Industry*. Madison: University of Wisconsin Press, 1987.

Barbour, Alan G. *John Wayne*. Pyramid, 1974.

Barnard, Edward S., ed. *Story of the Great American West*. Pleasantville, N.Y.: Reader's Digest Association, 1977.

Bayer, William. *The Great Movies*. New York: Ridge/Grosset and Dunlap, 1973.

Behlmer, Rudy. *America's Favorite Movies: Behind the Scenes*. New York: Ungar, 1982.

Bishop, George. *John Wayne: The Actor, the Man*. Caroline House, 1979.

Blake, Michael. *Dances with Wolves: A Novel*. New York: Ballantine, 1988.

Bleeker, Sonia. *The Sioux Indians: Hunters and Warriors of the Plains*. New York: Morrow, 1962.

Bosworth, Patricia. *Montgomery Clift: A Biography*. San Francisco: Harcourt Brace Jovanovich, 1978.

Brode, Douglas. *The Films of the Fifties*. Secaucus, N.J.: Citadel, 1976.

_____. *The Films of the Sixties*. Secaucus, N.J.: Citadel, 1980.

Brynner, Rock. *Yul: The Man Who Would Be King*. New York: Simon and Schuster, 1989.

Calder, Jenni. *There Must Be a Lone Ranger*. New York: Taplinger, 1974.

Canutt, Yakima, with Oliver Drake. *Stunt Man: The Autobiography of Yakima Canutt*. New York: Walker, 1979.

Carter, Alden R. *Last Stand at the Alamo*. New York: Franklin Watts/First Book, 1990.

Chase, Borden. *The Chisholm Trail*. Saturday Evening Post, 1946/47.

Clapham, Walter C. *Western Movies*. Octopus, 1974.

Clinch, Minty. *Burt Lancaster*. New York: Stein and Day, 1984.

Collins, James L. *Lawmen of the Old West*. New York: Franklin Watts/First Book, 1990.

Cook, David A. *A History of Narrative Film*. New York: Norton, 1981.

Costner, Kevin, Michael Blake and Jim Wilson. *Dances with Wolves: The Illustrated Story of the Epic Film*. New York: Newmarket, 1990.

Coursodon, Jean-Pierre, with Pierre Sauvage. *American Directors—Volumes I and II*. New York: McGraw-Hill, 1983.

Crowther, Bosley. *The Great Films: Fifty Golden Years of Motion Pictures*. New York: Putnam, 1967.

Current Biography Yearbook. New York: Wilson, published annually.

Dickens, Homer. *The Films of Gary Cooper*. Secaucus, N.J.: Citadel, 1970.

Durham, Philip, and Everett L. Jones. *The Negro Cowboys.* Lincoln: First Bison/University of Nebraska Press, 1983.

Eastman, John. *Retakes: Behind the Scenes of 500 Classic Movies.* New York: Ballantine, 1989.

Everson, William K. *The Hollywood Western: 90 Years of Cowboys and Indians, Train Robbers, Sheriffs and Gunslingers, and Assorted Heroes and Desperados.* Secaucus, N.J.: Citadel, 1969, 1992.

Fenin, George N., and William K. Everson. *The Western: From Silents to the Seventies (Revised Edition).* New York: Penguin, 1977.

Fisher, Leonard Everett. *The Alamo.* New York: Holiday House, 1987.

Forbis, William H. *The Old West: The Cowboys.* New York: Time-Life, 1973.

Ford, Dan. *Pappy: The Life of John Ford.* Englewood Cliffs, N.J.: Prentice-Hall, 1979.

Fraser, George MacDonald. *The Hollywood History of the World.* New York: Beech Tree/Morrow, 1988.

Gallagher, Tag. *John Ford: The Man and His Films.* Berkeley: University of California Press, 1986.

Gebert, Michael. *The Encyclopedia of Movie Awards.* New York: St. Martin's, 1996.

Goldman, William. *Adventures in the Screen Trade: A Personal View of Hollywood and Screenwriting.* New York: Warner, 1983.

Griggs, John. *The Films of Gregory Peck.* Secaucus, N.J.: Citadel, 1984.

Guerra, Mary Ann Noonan. *The Alamo.* Alamo, 1983.

Hamilton, John R. *Thunder in the Dust: Classic Images of Western Movies.* Text by John Calvin Batchelor. New York: Stewart, Tabori & Chang, 1987.

Hardy, Phil. *The Encyclopedia of Western Movies.* Woodbury, 1984.

Horan, James D. *The Gunfighters: The Authentic Wild West.* New York: Crown, 1976.

International Dictionary of Films and Filmmakers. Vol. 2: Directors. Detroit: St. James/Gale, 1984. *Vol. 3: Actors and Actresses.* Detroit: St. James/Gale, 1986. *Vol. 4: Writers and Production Artists.* Detroit: St. James/Gale, 1987.

Jackson, Ronald. *Classic TV Westerns.* Secaucus, N.J.: Citadel, 1994.

Jordan, Rene. *Gary Cooper.* Pyramid, 1974.

Keith, Todd. *Kevin Costner.* Ikonprint, 1991.

LaGuardia, Robert. *Monty: A Biography of Montgomery Clift.* New York: Arbor House, 1977.

Lake, A.I. *Gold Fever: The Wild West in American History.* Rourke, 1990.

Lake, Stuart N. *Wyatt Earp: Frontier Marshal.* Boston: Houghton Mifflin, 1931; reprint, Pocket, 1994.

L'Amour, Louis. *How the West Was Won.* New York: Bantam, 1963.

Landau, Elaine. *The Sioux.* New York: Franklin Watts/First Book, 1989.

Landry, J.C. *Paul Newman: An Illustrated Biography.* New York: McGraw-Hill, 1983.

LeMay, Alan. *The Searchers.* New York: Harper and Row, 1954.

Lenihan, John H. *Showdown: Confronting Modern America in the Western Film.* Urbana: University of Illinois Press, 1980.

How the West Was Won. By the editors of *Life* magazine. 1959.

Linet, Beverly. *Ladd: The Life, The Legend, The Legacy of Alan Ladd.* New York: Arbor House, 1979.

Lloyd, Ann, ed. *Movies of the Fifties.* Mary Knoll, N.Y.: Orbis, 1982.

_____. *Movies of the Forties.* Mary Knoll, N.Y.: Orbis, 1982.

_____. *Movies of the Silent Years.* Mary Knoll, N.Y.: Orbis, 1984.

_____. *Movies of the Sixties.* Mary Knoll, N.Y.: Orbis, 1983.

_____. *Movies of the Thirties.* Mary Knoll, N.Y.: Orbis, 1983.

Lyons, Grant. *Mustangs, Six Shooters and Barbed Wire: How the West Was Really Won.* New York: Julian Messner/Simon and Schuster, 1981.

McBride, Joseph. *Hawks on Hawks*. Berkeley: University of California Press, 1982.

McBride, Joseph, and Michael Wilmington. *John Ford*. New York: Da Capo, 1975.

McDonald, Archie P., ed. *Shooting Stars: Heroes and Heroines of Western Film*. Bloomington: Indiana University Press, 1987.

McKinney, Doug. *Sam Peckinpah*. Boston: Twayne, 1979.

Marrin, Albert. *Cowboys, Indians, and Gunfighters: The Story of the Cattle Kingdom*. New York: Atheneum, 1993.

Mast, Gerald. *Howard Hawks, Storyteller*. New York: Oxford University Press, 1982.

Matthews, Leonard. *History of Western Movies*. Los Angeles: Crescent, 1984.

May, Robin. *The Story of the Wild West*. New York: Hamlyn, 1978.

Michael, Paul. *The Academy Awards: A Pictorial History*. 5th ed. New York: Crown, 1982.

_____, ed. *The American Movies Reference Book*. Englewood Cliffs, N.J.: Prentice-Hall, 1969.

Morella, Joe, and Edward Z. Epstein. *Paul and Joanne: A Biography of Paul Newman and Joanne Woodward*. New York: Delacorte Press, 1988.

Navasky, Victor S. *Naming Names*. New York: Viking, 1980.

Norman, Barry. *The Story of Hollywood*. New York: NAL, 1987.

Oakley, J. Ronald. *God's Country: America in the Fifties*. Dambner, 1986.

Oumano, Elena. *Paul Newman*. New York: St. Martin's, 1989.

Parish, James Robert, and Michael R. Pitts. *The Great Western Pictures*. Metuchen, N.J.: Scarecrow, 1976.

_____, and Don E. Stanke. *The All-Americans*. New Rochelle, N.Y.: Arlington House, 1977.

Parkinson, Michael, and Clyde Jeavons. *A Pictorial History of Westerns*. New York: Hamlyn, 1972.

Peary, Danny. *Cult Movies*. New York: Delta Dell, 1981.

_____. *Cult Movies 3*. New York: Simon and Schuster, 1988.

Pfeiffer, Lee *The John Wayne Scrapbook*. Secaucus, N.J.: Citadel, 1991.

Place, Janey Ann. *The Western Films of John Ford*. Secaucus, N.J.: Citadel, 1974.

Poague, Leland A. *Howard Hawks*. Boston: Twayne, 1982.

Pronzini, Bill, and Martin H. Greenberg. *The Reel West: Classic Stories That Inspired Classic Films*. New York: Doubleday, 1984.

Pronzini, Bill, and Martin H. Greenberg, eds. *The Western Hall of Fame*. New York: Morrow, 1984.

Quirk, Lawrence J. *The Complete Films of William Holden*. Secaucus, N.J.: Citadel, 1986.

_____. *The Films of Paul Newman*. Secaucus, N.J.: Citadel, 1971.

Ricci, Mark, Boris Zmijewsky, and Steve Zmijewsky. *The Films of John Wayne*. Secaucus, N.J.: Citadel, 1970.

Richards, Norman V. *Cowboy Movies*. Lincoln: Bison University of Nebraska Press, 1984.

Rollings, Willard H. *The Comanche*. New York: Chelsea House, 1989.

Sackett, Susan. *The Hollywood Reporter Book of Box Office Hits*. New York: Billboard/Watson-Guptill, 1990.

St. Charnez, Casey. *The Films of Steve McQueen*. Secaucus, N.J.: Citadel Press, 1984.

Schaefer, Jack. *Shane*. Boston: Houghton Mifflin, 1949.

Scullin, George. "The Killer." *Holiday*, 1954.

Sennett, Ted. *Hollywood's Golden Year, 1939*. New York: St. Martin's, 1989.

Seydor, Paul. *Peckinpah: The Western Films*. Urbana: University of Illinois Press, 1980.

Shipman, David. *The Great Movie Stars: The International Years*. New York: St. Martin's, 1972.

Shores, Edward. *George Roy Hill*. Boston: Twayne, 1983.

Silver, Charles. *The Western Film*. Pyramid, 1976.

Simmons, Garner. *A Portrait in Montage: Peckinpah.* Austin: University of Texas Press, 1976.

Sinclair, Andrew. *John Ford.* New York: Dial, 1979.

Spada, James. *The Films of Robert Redford (Updated Edition).* Secaucus, N.J.: Citadel, 1984.

Tanner, Ogden. *The Old West: The Ranchers.* New York: Time-Life, 1977.

Terrill, Marshall. *Steve McQueen: Portrait of an American Rebel.* New York: Fine, 1993.

Thomas, Bob. *Golden Boy: The Untold Story of William Holden.* New York: St. Martin's, 1983.

Thomas, Tony. *Burt Lancaster.* Pyramid, 1975.

_____. *The Films of Kirk Douglas.* Secaucus, N.J.: Citadel, 1972.

_____. *The Great Adventure Films.* Secaucus, N.J.: Citadel, 1980.

Van Gelder, Peter. *That's Hollywood: A Behind-the-scenes Look at 60 of the Greatest Films Ever Made.* New York: Harper Perennial, 1990.

Wayne, Aissa, with Steve Delsohn. *John Wayne: My Father.* New York. Random House, 1991.

Wayne, Pilar, with Alex Thorleifson. *John Wayne: My Life with the Duke.* New York: McGraw-Hill, 1987.

Wiley, Mason, and Damien Bona. *Inside Oscar: The Unofficial History of the Academy Awards.* 4th ed. New York: Ballantine, 1986.

Wills, Charles A. *The Battle of the Little Bighorn.* New York: Silver Burdett/Simon and Schuster, 1990.

Zmijewsky, Boris, and Lee Pfeiffer. *The Films of Clint Eastwood.* Secaucus, N.J.: Citadel, 1982.

INDEX